THE INFINITE LOSS

By

Russell Harris

Grosvenor House
Publishing Limited

The right of Russell Harris to be identified as the author of this
work has been asserted in accordance with Section 78
of the Copyright, Designs and Patents Act 1988

The book cover picture is copyright to Russell Harris

This book is published by
Grosvenor House Publishing Ltd
28-30 High Street, Guildford, Surrey, GU1 3EL.
www.grosvenorhousepublishing.co.uk

A CIP record for this book
is available from the British Library

ISBN 978-1-78148-951-2

Dedicated to Ian and Fay Harris

Preface

As I start on the journey of writing this book I am at home looking out the window on a sunny summer's day in 2015. It is peaceful, pleasant and warm – a stark contrast to most of what follows. The majority of the story that will unfold covers the period from 2006 to 2012.

Benjamin Franklin famously said *"In this world nothing can be said to be certain, except death and taxes."* Certainly the loss of a loved one, especially a mother or father, is probably one of the most traumatic episodes a person will experience in their lifetime. Not only does the event have a unique intensity at the time, but can leave a dramatic change in the person and wider family left behind as an ongoing legacy.

A loss of any family member, particularly a parent, is a totally personal and specific emotional event for any individual. In every case the relationship between those two people is unique and no one else in the world can fully understand, appreciate or feel the same way. However, having said that, (as Benjamin Franklin eluded to) losing a parent is also a virtually universal event that we will all experience at some point in our lives – crossing the boundaries of geography, gender, age, race, belief systems etc.

Ever since I lost my mother back in 2006 I have felt the driving necessity to put pen to paper about my specific story. To share it with the wider world, not to elicit any sympathy but to allow one of billions of such situations to be captured for posterity and to share my generic views and reflections on such situations. Hopefully, the latter may elicit an association with the reader's own experiences to date and bring a certain comfort in the knowledge of people's commonality and universality. For those yet to succumb to such an experience my hope is that it provides a straw to hold onto when the inevitable happens and provides some thoughts and options for coping with the associated traumas.

Rather than set out the story and then save all the reflections, thoughts and views to the end I have tried to intersperse many of these at appropriate points in the various chapters – standing back/taking time out at key moments (albeit retrospectively). The epilogue is mainly reserved for more generic reflections and wider questions, some of which still remain unanswered.

Along the way I hope you come to know something about the wonderful individuals who were Ian and Fay, or for those who already knew them gain an even closer insight into their trials, struggles and virtues.

The journey that will unfold in the following pages was not taken alone (such journeys never are). The other person that has felt the pain as intensely as I have (if not more so) is my older sister Jacqueline. Without her I probably would not be sat here now with my sanity (fairly well) intact, recounting the events of the last few years. Also, I cannot thank my wife Linda enough for her fierce devotion and support through all the dark times. Other individuals will come to light throughout the story and for all the love, support, understanding and guidance given – not just to Jacqueline and I, but also to mum and dad – my enduring thanks and appreciation will always go out to you.

Prologue

So who were Ian and Fay Harris and their son and daughter, Russell and Jacqueline?

Fay Harris was born Fay Lee in West Hartlepool, Durham on 8th March 1915. She was the eldest daughter of Joe and Esther Lee, who were in the tailoring business and ran their own gown shop in West Hartlepool.

She helped bring up her youngest sister Lila, who was ten years younger than her (Esther had lost a child at birth five years after Fay was born) and worked in her parents' shop until they all moved to Leeds at the outbreak of the Second World War.

It was in Leeds on a foggy night that she happened to meet Ian on New Years' eve. They always used to joke about meeting "in the fog". They were married on 9th June 1948 and spent a lifetime together until 2006 (58 years of marriage). Lila and Ian's older brother Solly also got married – so two brothers married two sisters (kept the family intimate)!

Jacqueline was born on 2nd May 1950 and I was born four years later on 29th November 1954. Fay was a wonderfully traditional and loving wife and mother, carrying out that role full time whilst Jacqueline and I were in our formative school years. Only when I was in my mid-teens did she go back to work part time (in a card shop in central Leeds), mainly to enable the family to afford those little extras, including going on package holidays together in the summer.

Like a lot of Jewish mothers she had her culinary specialities – none more so than a memorable apple pie. Her nephews David and Leslie used to drop in regularly just to "sample" the latest batch of pies.

Unfortunately, her sister Lila was taken from her at the early age of forty nine after a prolonged battle with cancer and numerous operations to try to stem the spread.

Despite becoming nearly deaf in the later years of her life and having poor sight and mobility she (like Ian) never complained and always maintained a wonderful sense of humour.

To Fay, family was everything and she is as deeply missed now as she was on that traumatic day of her passing nine years ago.

Ian was born in Melbourne, Australia as Isadore Harris on 16th October 1917 to Sam and Rose Harris (who had emigrated from England). He had an older brother Solly and a younger brother Myer.

Although he spent his early years in Melbourne the family returned to England when Ian was in his early teens and settled in Leeds.

He went to Lovell Road School and won a scholarship to the Royal College of Arts in London; obtained his degree from Royal College and won a prize giving him a travelling scholarship in design. Unfortunately, the outbreak of the war precluded him from taking this up. All three brothers fought in World War II. Myer was shot down and killed over Dusseldorf on a bombing raid – something with which Ian always found difficulty in coming to terms.

His parents returned to Australia, but having met his future wife Fay, Ian and his remaining brother Solly stayed in Leeds.

He changed his name to Ian Miles Harris by deed poll in 1956 (having been given some advice) adopting the middle name in memory of his late younger brother, Myer. As mentioned above Fay and Ian were married in Leeds in 1948.

After the war Ian initially went into the furniture making business and then turned to teaching. He progressed to becoming headmaster of Cleckheaton County Secondary School, which became West End Middle School – (then) the largest middle school in Yorkshire. He remained headmaster for many years until his early retirement (due to ill health) at the age of sixty in 1977.

He was a leading light both in the NAS/UWT (National Association of Schoolmasters/Union of Women Teachers) and the NAHT (National Association of Head Teachers) and his contributions were recognised by being awarded Life Membership of both of these associations.

As a religious person he also played a major part in the Jewish community in Leeds (and nationally) – his grandfather was the first Jewish butcher in Leeds. One of many things he achieved included arranging the move of a major synagogue in Leeds (the Chassidishe in Spencer Place), using his own house as collateral for the transaction! Again his major contributions were recognised by this synagogue when they made him Life President.

As part of Jewish Board of Deputies he once had the honour of meeting the Queen in London. She asked him which side he wanted to win in the forthcoming England v

Australia cricket test match; Ian answered "either side as long as it is a good game" to which the Queen replied "Mr Harris you should have become a diplomat"!

Ian came relatively late to masonic activity. He was initiated at Legiolium Lodge (No. 1542) in Castleford on 16th June 1975. As with all the other endeavours in his life, he gave his all to masonry and became Master of Legiolium Lodge in October 1991. His Masonic work was also recognised in May 1999 when he received provincial honours – becoming Past Provincial Assistant Grand Registrar in Yorkshire.

A sudden heart attack in August 1975 robbed Ian of his remaining brother, Solly. Ian increasingly looked after Fay in later years due to her failing health – she always said that between the two of them he was the better cook!

Ian and Fay always lived in Leeds after they were married. My first memory was that of our four bed semi-detached home at 10 Harrogate Road in the Chapeltown area. We had many happy years there until both Jacqueline and I finally left home. After dad retired they downsized to a two bedroom first floor flat in the Alwoodley area of Leeds – 3 Cresta Court, Primley Park Garth. Both of their nephews (Lila and Solly's children) – Leslie and David – lived in the same area and they were fortunate in having a number of good neighbours in the cul-de-sac where they lived (plus one or two awkward ones as well – c'est la vie)! Some of these close neighbours will feature at times in the story ahead. Moira and David Gelman came from South Africa and lived in a house across the road with their daughter Haddassah and son Jessie; the next house to them had Paul and Debbie Jacobson and family (Paul being a solicitor by profession); then there was Lou and Pearl Stoller along with their daughter Freda-Eve in the house adjacent to the three flats that comprised Cresta Court.

Over the years health problems inevitably raised their heads; more seriously for Ian than for Fay. Ian's issues in later life probably started when he collapsed at school when he was fifty eight. After investigations in hospital the final prognosis was hypertension and over-work. He was never the same health wise after that and took early retirement two years later at the age of sixty. Over the ensuing years he suffered increasingly from heart and angina problems resulting in open heart bypass surgery at Killingbeck Hospital in Leeds in April 1992. Mr Nair, the surgeon who carried out the operation, indicated that the expected life of the bypass was ten to fifteen years – a time that was to be far exceeded in reality (a theme that will recur throughout this book, with Ian "beating the odds" on many an occasion). Further health problems followed, with Ian having to have his gall bladder removed in December 1997 and breaking his femur in a fall in March 2002. Angina issues continued for the rest of his life – despite the bypass surgery – unfortunately being "unstable" rather than "stable" in nature (stable angina is generally brought on by over exertion, whereas the unstable type can occur at any time – even at rest in a chair – and is therefore more unpredictable, unexpected and more difficult to treat).

Fortunately Fay did not suffer the fate of needing major surgery like Ian, but suffered from declining health in an equally debilitating if not acute manner. Hearing loss had been a problem for many years. I remember as a child holding her hand and talking to her, with her saying "come round to the other side so I can hear you better". Over the years the hearing loss escalated until towards the end of her life (even with a strong hearing aid) it was very difficult for her to hear – resulting in a degree of isolation no one with reasonable hearing can truly comprehend. As often accompanied by age, her eyesight also deteriorated substantially – despite a cataract operation. A larger TV screen (with associated larger subtitles) and the best spectacle prescription helped to some degree but her eyesight was still poor in later years. Mobility became the other main physical issue with major problems with her knees etc. A fall in the flat in May 2001 resulted in a broken hip which reduced her to using a Zimmer frame about the home and effectively meant she needed a wheelchair when she went out. At that stage the pressure was increased on Ian as he had to take over responsibility for most day to day activities i.e. cooking, shopping, ironing etc.

Despite all of the above one of the most remarkable things was that neither Ian nor Fay ever complained about what happened to them and their situation. They always kept their strong sense of humour throughout these difficult years.

Turning to the other two pieces of the jigsaw – there was Jacqueline and I. Jacqueline was also born in Leeds, went through school, attending Allerton High School taking GCSE "O" and "A" levels (showing our age). She originally started teacher training college, but decided that was not for her and joined Barclays Bank. Her real love was theatre and the stage, having taken ballet and a myriad of other dance classes over the years. She was also a member of some of the top amateur operatic societies in Leeds who staged highly professional productions at the Grand Theatre (the home of English National Opera North). In her early twenties she decided to turn professional as a singer and dancer resulting in summer shows, pantomimes and other professional engagements around the country – effectively leaving home (just returning in between engagements).

Over the years obtaining professional engagements became more difficult and in 1985 she had a complete career change joining British Airways as a Customer Services Agent, working in Terminal 1 at Heathrow (I had joined British Airways five years earlier as will be explained below). Thus, the Greater London area became her first home away from home, purchasing a flat in Windermere Way, West Drayton, Middlesex. She stayed with British Airways for twenty four years until she gave up work in 2009, progressing through the ranks to hold positions such as Duty Manager in the terminals etc.

She married Andreas Panayiotidis in February 1990 and eventually moved to a house in Bagshot, Surrey where she lives to this day (only a few minutes' drive from where I live in West End).

Finally there is the author – yours truly. I had a wonderful childhood in Leeds starting school at Chapeltown County Primary School (a short walk from the house on Harrogate Road) and progressing through Roundhay Grammar School. After GCSE "A" levels I went on to complete a BSc (Honours) degree in Mathematics at Leeds University.

I always wanted to go into aviation, but at the time of leaving university the airline business was going through one of its cyclical trough periods with minimal recruitment, so in the interim I decided to take the opportunity to obtain a professional business qualification with a view to knocking on the door of the airline businesses at a later stage. I joined Coopers & Lybrand (to merge into PwC in later years) in their Leeds office and spent three years becoming a Chartered Accountant (fortunately passing the exams first time – I couldn't bear the thought of having to do any re-sits).

By the time I qualified the airline sector had picked up and I applied and was successful in obtaining a position in British Airways audit department in London starting on 3rd March 1980 at Bealine House, South Ruislip. So, at last, the final bird flew the nest at the age of twenty five, with Ian and Fay in their early/mid-sixties.

I was fortunate to have a fascinating and successful career with British Airways for twenty six years until I took early retirement in 2006 - holding thirteen roles over those years, including several senior management positions. The diverse roles took me all over the world on business and with the excellent travel concessions, allowed me to travel just as extensively for pleasure. For many years I had mum, dad and Jacqueline named on my concessions which allowed us to experience exotic, wonderful holidays together all over the world – from North America to Rio de Janeiro, Dubai to Kenya; Hong Kong to Australia and most points in between. Being able to take mum and dad first class on many occasions gave me real pleasure in being able to give something back after all the decades of them bringing me up and giving me everything. During my career British Airways also sponsored me for their Senior Management Academy resulting in my obtaining an MBA qualification from Lancaster University.

After one or two temporary haunts I eventually bought a one bedroom flat in Yeading, Middlesex where I stayed for a number of years until moving to the Woking area of Surrey (as I was working at Gatwick at the time). It was in 1992, in Guildford, that I met Linda Taylor – my wife to be. Although we did not get married until 2007 we have been together ever since that first meeting in Guildford and since April 2000 have lived in a house in West End – a village mid-way between Woking and Camberley.

As a family we were always very close, with constant contact with mum and dad even when Jacqueline and I had moved away from home. We would always call home at least once a week if not more often and go back to mum and dad's place in Leeds at least once a month (even more often in the early years). As mentioned above, even as adults we still enjoyed family holidays together and have a wealth of wonderful memories from those times. To this day I could not imagine a better set of parents. Mum was the ideal mother with a fierce, all consuming love and support for her family and dad was a complete "role model" to me as a person, father and mentor. No doubt the fact that I view them in this way made the events that follow all that more traumatic and painful.

Chapter 1

Some time ago a friend of mine forwarded to me an email which crystallises the way life unfolds. The years from 2006 to 2012 were to bring these sentiments into sharp focus:

"Life is like a journey on a train...with its stations... with changes of routes...and with accidents!

At birth we boarded the train and met our parents, and we believe they will always travel on our side.

However, at some station our parents will step down from the train, leaving us on this journey alone.

As time goes by, other people will board the train; and they will be significant i.e. our siblings, friends, children, and even the love of our life.

Many will step down and leave a permanent vacuum. Others will go so unnoticed that we don't realise that they vacated their seats!

This train ride will be full of joy, sorrow, fantasy, expectations, hellos, goodbyes, and farewells.

Success consists of having a good relationship with all passengers...requiring that we give the best of ourselves.

The mystery to everyone is we do not know at which station we ourselves will step down. So, we must live in the best way – love, forgive, and offer the best of who we are.

It is important to do this because when the time comes for us to step down and leave our seat empty — we should leave behind beautiful memories for those who will continue to travel on the train of life".

Sunday 26th February 2006 started off as any other Sunday. Linda and I went down to the health club we were members of in West Byfleet – Linda did her gym workout and I attended an advanced step class I had been doing for years. We got home around lunchtime as normal and had a bite to eat.

That weekend was one where my sister Jacqueline was in Leeds with mum and dad (we each tended to go up once a month, so generally there was one of us there every couple of weeks). I rang early afternoon as normal and got to chat with dad about the myriad of things we would normally cover. It seemed a normal conversation, the like of which we had had hundreds of times before. There was no indication of what was about to happen next.

A little while later the phone rang and I picked it up – it was Jacqueline at the other end. Dad had suffered a severe angina/heart attack at the flat and the ambulance crew were there in attendance, intending to take him in to St James's Hospital in Leeds. Unfortunately, due to the experiences of dad's illnesses over the years, I switched into "automatic" mode in terms of what to do next. I said to Jacqueline that I would pack and drive up to Leeds straight away; we agreed to talk on my way up when matters were clearer.

I spent the next half hour or so going through the (well worn) motions of getting my case down from the loft, packing everything I might need (assuming this could go on for some time rather than a day or two) and collecting work related items, as I would need to contact my boss/staff the next day and talk through what would need to be done (once we were clearer about dad's situation).

The drive up to Leeds normally took about three and a half hours. As in the past, it proved a surreal and anxious time – time for the mind to trawl through all the possibilities that Jacqueline and I might be faced with in this situation; practicalities of ensuring mum was looked after if dad was going to be in hospital/ incapacitated for some time etc. At the back of my mind there were always the flashes of the thought – could this be an episode too far (dad was eighty eight after all, with a long history of medical problems and challenges). As most people would probably do, I tried to lock that particular avenue of thought back in its box, certainly until an initial indication of the severity of dad's condition was clearer.

The exact order and timing of events in Leeds are somewhat hazy now as I try to recall them. Moira Gelman had come over to the flat from across the road to stay with mum until we knew what was happening (as Jacqueline had obviously gone to hospital along with the ambulance).

The outcome was that they admitted dad and he ended up in what could best be described as a geriatric ward – most of the people appeared much older than him, albeit in terms of age they were probably not. For an eighty eight year old he was still an amazingly bright, articulate, intelligent, astute and sociable individual – most people usually guessed he was in his sixties when they met him. Looking back the ward atmosphere was certainly not conducive to recovery for someone like Ian – apart from the determination to get the hell out of there!

Glossing over the blow by blow events, the final diagnosis was that Ian had suffered another extreme angina attack rather than an actual heart attack. He was already on a plethora of medication, albeit the doctors reviewed the dosages again due to the latest incident. After a short period in hospital they decided to discharge Ian. I agreed with Jacqueline that I would stay on for a while until, hopefully, dad recovered his strength etc., (this latest episode had hit him hard, physically) and she should go back to London/work – we could discuss swapping around again over the following few days.

What became rapidly apparent once dad was home was that all was definitely *not* well. Having some angina pains from time to time had, unfortunately, become a way of life for dad over recent years. He had a pre-scribed GTN spray (glyceride tri-nitrate) which he always kept in his pocket. He would spray a couple of times under his tongue whenever he felt an angina episode coming on. This helped to dilate the blood vessels, improving blood flow to the heart and hence reducing/extinguishing the pain. Despite not exerting himself at home we found that even getting ready for bed often left him with the start of chest pains and the need to use the GTN spray – this was an unusual turn compared with the past.

Before long another major attack ensued. Dad had gone to bed early one night and suddenly the extreme pain came on. Despite three sets of sprays at intervals of a few minutes the situation was getting worse rather than better. Ian was banging his chest asking for the pain to stop. There was no choice but to ring 999 again and get an ambulance (with the inevitable consequences of a hospital re-admission). Mum had been getting ready for bed and I asked her to go into the living room – seeing dad in such distress (again) would not be good for her health either (she had suffered from high blood pressure in the past). After ringing for the emergency services I rang Moira again and explained the situation – she said she would be right over, despite the late hour, and would look after mum for however long was necessary.

In retrospect, I have a couple of reflections on what was happening at that time. Firstly, minutes seem like hours when you are waiting for medical assistance in these situations – albeit they were probably there within ten minutes. It is not so much the advent of the situation itself that is so traumatic, but the feeling of helplessness and seeing a loved one in such obvious extreme pain and distress. All that anyone can do is to try and make the right decision (to call for professional help), try and comfort/talk to the person themselves so they don't feel so alone and that help is imminent, and also to try and isolate any other people that would be traumatically affected so they don't have to see/experience the anxiety and stress. Secondly, it brings home how fortunate you are if there are other family members or friends there to help and alleviate some of the worry, so you can concentrate on the person who is ill (knowing mum would be looked after whilst the situation with dad resolved itself was a big help).

The situation of 26th February was reversed with my calling Jacqueline to let her know the situation and she indicated she would be back up straight away.

Over the following day or so back in the "geriatric" ward at St James's Hospital dad's situation was perplexing the doctor's until one of the senior consultants attended and reviewed his case. We were all visiting dad at the time (mum, Jacqueline and I) when the senior consultant asked to talk to us. Jacqueline and I stepped away with her to a more private part of the ward. She was a charming lady, but what she was about to say would shock us all. She explained that the underlying medical issue was *NOT* dad's heart/angina – but that she believed he had kidney (renal) failure!! She went on to explain that, perversely, with the kidneys having little function left the heart was trying to "compensate" in terms of other functions the body requires and that this strain was what was causing the repeated and increasingly severe attacks.

Having been told what was wrong, Jacqueline and I immediately asked the obvious question – so what is the suggested treatment? She indicated that there was only one course of treatment – he would need to go on kidney dialysis for the rest of his life – and as soon as possible! It is at these times that you go cold out of the shock of the diagnosis and implications. We all went back to dad's bedside where he was sat up on the edge of the bed talking to mum. The consultant sat down and took dad through what she had told us. I always remember that one of the first questions dad asked her was what would happen if he didn't go onto dialysis – she simply said that he would die within a relatively short time!!

In all my life I had only seen an immensely strong man in my father. He had a phenomenal strength of mind to cope with whatever life had thrown at him and the determination and willpower to get through/recover from anything that happened to him. For the first time that mould was broken. As I looked at him sat on the edge of the bed he was visibly shaking with the impact of the news. In those few moments all our lives changed forever.

After time to think about the consequences Ian agreed to go ahead with dialysis, having being told the outline of what that would entail. Initially he would need two tubes inserted either in the groin region or at the base of the neck, where they could attach the dialysis machines. He would need to attend dialysis three times a week (at St James's Hospital) for around three and a half hours per session (plus setting up/taking off time). Over time it may be possible to have a procedure to create a fistula (which I will cover later) which would mean the external tubes could be removed – but dialysis was now for life (however long that might be).

I cannot remember now whether it was at this time or later with one of dad's renal doctors that Jacqueline and I asked, on average (at dad's age) how long do people manage to survive on dialysis? The answer was approximately two years! Suddenly the future looked very different from a few weeks ago. As things played out we were fortunate to have dad with us for a considerably longer period of time (as I mentioned before, he had this incredible determination and resilience that resulted in him "beating the odds" on many an occasion).

The roller coaster that was health and hospitals had a further dip even at this early stage in the ride. Before the doctors could arrange the start of dialysis there was another attack, which resulted in dad being taken into the coronary care ward at the hospital. The situation was stabilised over a twenty four hour period and the doctors/nurses started to talk about moving him back to his original ward. When Jacqueline and I told dad the news he said he did not want to go back there – he would rather discharge himself and take the consequences of going home. It is likely that had we just blandly accepted his wishes this story would have ended shortly afterwards. We understood his attitude as in this weak state he no doubt felt that going back there was almost resigning himself to a possible death in an "old age" surrounding.

Instead of accepting this Jacqueline and I "went into battle" on his behalf – something that would happen on more than one occasion in the future (we make a formidable team in these situations – Jacqueline always says that she is the "heart" (emotional one) and I am the "head" (logical one) in these circumstances). In summary, we spent a considerable time talking to both the ward sister and the doctors about the situation, impressing on them Ian's fighting spirit and the fact that this was a very unusual attitude from him brought about by the undesirable nature of the ward he had been on. To cut a long story short the ward sister finally agreed to hold him in coronary care for a further night and look to try and get him moved directly on to a renal ward to expedite the necessary move to dialysing him – we had won this initial battle.

The renal ward (Ward 57) was different class. Bright, airy and spacious with people of all ages there. We were even allowed to bring in the duvet from the bed at home which just made things feel that bit more personal. You actually felt it was a stopping point to going home, rather than a stopping point to ....

However, the first attempt at dialysis did not go well – they found it difficult to get lines into the vein in the groin, so decided to switch to putting in a Tesio line in the base of the neck. This meant there were two plastic tubes that protruded a few inches from the bottom of the neck near the collar bone (with "stops" on the end). Under the surface the tubes went into blood vessels. When not in use the lines would be wrapped up and just rest on the upper chest (so you could wear a shirt as normal). Once these were in place the never ending round of weekly dialysis started with sessions on Tuesday, Thursday and Saturday. In theory one might think of dialysis as a benign process – after all, a person just sits/lies there whilst the blood is cleaned and all the toxins removed by a machine (substituting for the functions of the kidneys). However, in reality this process puts a significant strain on the body. Blood pressure invariably dips during the process – something that would prove an extreme challenge in later years as dad already had low(ish) blood pressure – and it tends to leave most people feeling drained and extremely tired afterwards. We (and I am sure Ian) didn't realise it at the time but he had done a number of things (we all take for granted) for the last time i.e. driving a car, shopping, making meals etc.

As in the past, we thought we may have hit rock bottom and were on the way back up. However nothing was more true than that famous saying *"just when you think it's safe to go back in the water ...."*.

Back at the flat Jacqueline and I were taking care of mum, bringing her in to see Ian on a regular basis. One night we were all in mum and dad's bedroom with mum sat on a chair getting ready for bed. We were helping her get changed and all talking when suddenly Fay said something to us that made no sense. Jacqueline looked at me and I looked at her and both our hearts sank. Fay said something else that didn't make sense! Jacqueline said to her that she was obviously very tired, so let us help her into bed where she could get a good night's sleep. Jacqueline and I were both thinking the same think, but said nothing until we were on our own ..... a stroke? She had been extremely stressed by all the events of the last couple of weeks and had admitted that seeing dad laid on the floor at home with the paramedics working on him, on that day back in February when this all started, made her think she was going to lose him at that point. Maybe this had all built up to the event we had just witnessed.

We held our breath, but fortunately next morning mum seemed to be back to her old self – talking normally, no physical effects etc. Had we dodged the bullet? The answer was to be an emphatic NO.

In hindsight, should we have done something different at the time the episode occurred? It is very easy to say, in the cold light of day and with future knowledge, that we should have called for an ambulance and had the possibility of a stroke explored straight away (catching these incidents very soon after they occur can reduce the impact significantly). Having said that, the level of immediate diagnosis and stroke care nearly ten years ago was not at the level it is nowadays. However, calling for an ambulance would have exacerbated mum's stress exponentially at that time and the thought of how to practically cope with both parents in hospital at the same time was frightening. Considering the morning seemed to bring back normality we carried on dealing with the challenges we were already facing. The calm was to prove short lived.

It's an observation on the events throughout this book that faced with stresses, challenges and decision points it is far too easy to look back and feel guilty about the decisions taken when you know how the future unfolds. All you can do is make the best informed decision you can, given all the facts and unique circumstances at the time. In this respect the words of Francis of Assisi come to mind, namely "... *grant me the strength to accept the things I cannot change, the courage to change the things I can, and the wisdom to know the difference.*"

Whilst dad was in hospital I had been looking for something at the flat and opened a drawer in a side table he had by his chair in the living room. To my amazement it was full of bills, letters etc. This was incredibly unusual as Ian had always been meticulous in dealing with paperwork, had a row of box files neatly arranged and labelled in the bookcase in the hall with everything filed precisely – a trait I inherited in spades (for which I will always be grateful). I spent an afternoon filing everything away and came across a notice indicating his car was due for an MOT – the date was the next day! I urgently had to contact the Ford garage he used, advise them of our home situation and sweet talk them into carrying out the MOT at very short notice. However, the real significance of the above was that it was obvious dad had got to the stage where he was finding it difficult to cope with day to day things as he had done in the past – yet he had never opened up on this subject to Jacqueline and I. As a reflection for others facing similar situations it is very easy to miss the small things that indicate there may be a larger underlying problem occurring. Always keep an eye out for anything that is slightly out of a person's routine or character – better to pick it up earlier rather than later.

After a period ensuring that the dialysis was progressing reasonably and that dad was stable, recovering from all the recent traumas, they let him home from St James's. It was obvious that he and mum would require much more support going forward in the short to medium term, and we started to research from where this might come. We made contact with Yorkshire Care (a private care company) to discuss our needs and what support they could offer. Fortunately over the years dad had built up savings which could prove a buffer and source to pay for the support he and/or mum might require in later life. However, the longer term solution would be quite different.

In the past Jacqueline and I had discussed with mum and dad the option of them selling up in Leeds and moving in with one of us in Surrey. Although they considered this seriously they had said it wasn't the right time – and they would let us know when they felt the time was appropriate. It was now crystal clear that the time had come – although the way this would play out was different from that first envisaged, for reasons that will become clear. Along similar lines, we also arranged a power of attorney for both mum and dad towards the end of March 2006, giving Jacqueline and I the ability to implement any actions they decided, i.e. setting up or changing bank/savings accounts, signing documents on their behalf etc. We were fortunate that Paul Jacobson who lived across the road from the flat in Leeds was a solicitor, so he gave us all the advice we required and arranged all the paperwork in quick time.

If I was to table any advice at this point I would encourage people who may be faced with such challenging situations to take this step earlier rather than later. It still leaves the person in charge of making the decisions, but allows family or friends to implement those decisions or wishes on their behalf and hence makes the practicalities much easier (when there may be other more intense stresses on the people involved). There is no need to gain any court approval at this stage – that is only required if the person were to lose their ability to make the initial decisions. Any local solicitor should be able to provide the paperwork/support for a reasonable charge.

Around the same time dad also made a small donation to the hospital (Ward 57) as a thank you for all their care and support – this was a typical appreciative and philanthropic gesture, as anyone who knew dad would tell you.

Throughout all the above, Jacqueline and I were trying to balance the situation in Leeds whilst still being employed by British Airways. We were both fortunate to have extremely understanding and supportive bosses, who were comfortable with us taking whatever time was necessary in order to cope with the problems. I was slightly more fortunate in that I had already agreed to take an early retirement package at the end of March.

Due to the issues we were facing there was a mutual agreement to extend this to the end of April, so I would be able to spend some time in the office finalising and handing over work before I finished (as I had spent very little time there in March as you can imagine). I had volunteered for the early retirement package before everything blew up on the family front in late February. I hadn't particularly been thinking about finishing at British Airways as I still loved working there, but the package on offer was extremely generous and I had started to realise that with mum and dad's advanced ages and deteriorating health I may need appreciable amounts of personal time in the not too distant future (though I hadn't realised how soon I would need it) – how prophetic that now seems to have been.

Jacqueline and I were now taking a few days in rotation to return to Surrey/work so there was always one of us in Leeds to look after things.

I want to return to the point about work and bosses/managers for a minute. One of the things that the above experiences crystallised for me is what a difference supportive managers can have on people coping with personal crises in their lives. Most people view managers as the people who organise, make decisions, enforce structure and rules etc. But the true "people" manager goes well beyond that. They realise that where their understanding and support is *most* needed by people who work for them is during the most difficult times. That is where they go the extra mile to alleviate whatever level of stress they can. They truly balance the needs of the individual with that of the organisation. Managers who act in this way (usually from a deep seated part of their own belief system) invariably find that their "investment" is rewarded many times over when a person returns to work. I can recall a couple of circumstances in the past as a senior manager myself where I tried to provide similar support to people trying to deal with their own major personal challenges – going the extra mile. But it wasn't until being on the receiving end of the experience that I truly appreciated what a great help and support that approach provided – a thought to ponder for those in authority.

Picking up the story again, I had returned home for a few days to catch up on matters, calling Leeds each day to check on how things were going. Suddenly the "roller coaster" took another lurch. Mum had experienced another, more serious, stroke/mini-stroke. Although her speech was still okay this latest episode had manifested itself as a physical, mobility problem. She now had extreme difficulty getting up and moving around (even with a Zimmer frame) and even if she was held up/supported by people she felt she was falling all the time (and would cry out to that effect). Jacqueline had called for support and the local emergency response team from social services had come out to help.

This latest turn for the worse had significant implications for looking after mum and dad. Getting in and out of bed was now extremely difficult for mum and resulted in the urgent purchase of a new bed that was higher and had space below, in case there was need for a hoist to be used going forwards. Going to the toilet (day or night) was now a major problem needing people to support her etc. Although the provision of a commode chair (next to the bed) helped, the underlying problems were extensive. Getting around the flat was now only really possible using a wheelchair. Social services did agree to arrange care workers to come in and help at regular intervals each day in terms of getting up/washed, going to the toilet and getting ready for bed, but in reality this proved to be a nightmare. Key issues were continuity, timing and quality. Very rarely did the same people come each day – so there was a constant need for briefing them, no building of a relationship/trust with Fay; the timing was as dictated by social services rather than what best suited the family e.g. they would say that they would have to come at some time like 7 p.m. to get her to bed – ridiculous; and the quality of staff was extremely variable.

In terms of the last point, I remember one incident when two care workers were in the bathroom one day with mum helping her wash etc. They were so busy trying to rattle through what they needed to do to get onto their next visit that they were extremely careless and didn't make sure that at least one of them had hold of Fay. She started to fall backwards and it was only by good fortune and timing that the bathroom door was open and I was passing. I caught her from the back as she was starting to fall. Again, in her current state this episode made her extremely anxious – she kept saying "I was falling". We tried to assure her that it was just her feeling that due to the stroke rather than the fact she was actually falling (a lie) – only because we were desperately trying to build her confidence back up. Suffice to say that as soon as these two workers had left we were on to the care services organisation – those two people never attended Fay again! We also started to pursue private support more intensely after this episode. It was an unfortunate truth, but at that time the only way to dictate as to the most appropriate support required was to pay for it privately – otherwise the system was not particularly patient centric and simply dictated to the individual and family what they would receive, and when, as a result of operational constraints.

As the end of April came my twenty six years with British Airways also came to an end. After so many years as a senior manager in the organisation it would have been satisfying to finish on a high. But I was only back for a couple of days at the end, so didn't have the time to do the extensive round of goodbyes I would have liked. Also, a number of senior colleagues had left on similar packages at the end of March and so were not around to attend my farewell presentation/ make appropriate speeches. After so many wonderful years it all ended as a bit of a damp squib.

I remember giving back my company car that last day and making my way over to the central area at Heathrow on a shuttle bus from Waterside (the British Airways business centre/head office). I picked up a coach that would take me back to Woking train station where Linda would pick me up. As the coach drove around the western perimeter road of Heathrow the sun was going down and I looked across the airport that had been at the heart of my career and it suddenly hit me – I no longer worked for British Airways. I could remember clearly my first day on joining and now twenty six years were over in a flash – I felt extremely sad inside (the first of what was to be a number of "losses").

The situation in Leeds did not change materially in the short term. Mum's capability improved a little over time but not significantly. The approach to dad's dialysis took a step forward in early May when he attended an appointment to have an ultrasound scan on his arm, with a view to creating a fistula for him. A fistula is formed by connecting an artery and a vein under the skin (normally in the forearm close to the wrist). When the artery and the vein are connected the pressure inside the vein increases which makes the vein stronger and bigger. Once the vein has had time to become strong (normally about 6 to 8 weeks after the procedure) two needles can be put into it each time as part of the dialysis process. One needle is used to take blood out to the machine whilst the other returns "cleaned" blood back to the body. Normally the procedure to create a fistula can be done under a local anaesthetic. The benefits of a fistula are that (a) the line/tubes in the neck can be removed, (b) there is a better quality of dialysis, (c) there is less chance of infection and (d) access is more reliable and lasts longer than other options. The prognosis was good and a schedule was proposed to carry out the procedure to create the fistula towards the end of June.

Returning to Fay, a pivotal event happened towards the end of May. It was not obvious when it happened exactly, but probably during the night as we became aware of the change over breakfast one day. Rather than sitting up at the main table we found that mum was more comfortable sitting in her armchair for meals using a tray table. We had prepared her breakfast as normal with juice, cereal, boiled egg etc., but we noticed very quickly that it was taking her all her time just to have a few mouthfuls of anything. As I was getting dad breakfast and having some myself I would see that every couple of minutes mum seemed to have almost dosed off – she was not staying "with us" for more than a short space of time! The result was that she was no longer able to eat very much (she probably had a quarter of her normal breakfast – at most – in about a period of an hour). To cut a long story short, we had the GP attend and he recommended that a consultant specialist dealing with geriatric conditions needed to see her as soon as possible.

Jacqueline and I were both there when the specialist came. After examining and assessing Fay she sat down and gave us her recommendation. She indicated that Fay would benefit from a short spell in hospital specifically to "start to get her back on her feet". When questioned by us on the length of stay she gave an indicative period of just a few days. It was obvious that something outside our capabilities needed to be done if mum was going to improve and so (reluctantly) we agreed. What transpired was a very different story from what was indicated (a learning point I will return to later).

The specialist arranged for an ambulance to come and pick mum up. When they did the scene was heart breaking. Despite trying to explain to mum what was happening and why (and that it should help her improve) she desperately did not want to leave Ian and go into hospital. As the ambulance men put her in a chair to take her down stairs (the flat was on the first floor) she stretched her arm out to dad who was sat in his chair (still looking frail due to the recent events/ dialysis) and kept saying "Ian, don't let them take me, don't let them take me". It must have been even more horrendous for dad than it was for Jacqueline and I. Little did we know at the time that mum would never return home to us.

They took her into St. James's Hospital (we seemed to have been spending our whole lives there over the previous few weeks). Over the next couple of days when we visited we started to realise that the hospital was not taking any positive action in the way we had been led to believe. Mum did open her eyes from time to time but was not really with us. She also seemed very restless the whole time – whether her eyes were open or not. We eventually tackled the medical staff and particularly raised the issue of her not really eating, so how was she to get nourishment. They did put up a drip in response to our questioning.

However, matters were brought to a head by us when we insisted on discussing her condition with the doctors involved. What they said came as a body blow to us all. Effectively they said there really was very little that they could do for Fay and the best they could do was to make her as comfortable as possible over the relatively short time left – we were all devastated. They agreed to move her into a private room where we could visit/stay at any time. Although nobody could be sure, the indication was that she probably only had up to a week left to live. The staff assured us that they would make her as comfortable as possible and use any appropriate drugs (e.g. morphine) to help in this respect.

At this juncture it is worth considering what happened when the specialist came out to see Fay and recommended a "few days" in hospital. Jacqueline and I have discussed this on more than one occasion since and still cannot conclude whether (a) she genuinely believed that there was treatment that could improve mum's condition, or (b) she saw the bigger picture of dad's situation and our trying to cope and took the decision that it would be beneficial overall to have a hospital bear the brunt of looking after Fay in her final days. If it was (a) then you have to question her judgement and/or communication with the doctor's looking after mum in the hospital. If it was (b) then I would purport that she overstepped her boundaries, taking such a decision without openly discussing the matter and options with the family. I am not sure what support might have been available to keep mum at home for her final days (if we had known the true position), but it is certainly something we would all have been strongly in favour of given the choice. In the end it was not a decision we were allowed to make (very different from what would happen to dad in the future).

I know from Jacqueline and I talking about the situation in the years since this time, that she carries a feeling of guilt around maybe not fighting hard enough for mum in hindsight – in somehow letting her down (and I must admit to getting such pangs myself from time to time). However, we learnt a great deal from looking after dad in the forthcoming years (as subsequent pages will set out) and I vehemently believe that given the same situation, with the same knowledge and experience (or lack of) as we had then and given the same advice we would have agreed to the same action.

The other thing I was to realise in hindsight (having subsequently gone to work for Monitor, the health sector regulator) was that St. James's Hospital was implementing the (now infamous) Liverpool Care Pathway. This was an approach to end of life care that has subsequently been questioned and superseded.

The next few days were obviously the hardest we had all faced as a family. In between his dialysis we took dad in to see mum a few times in a wheelchair (he was needing to use that more and more). He would sit, talk to her, hold her hand and sometimes tickle her palm – he said he often did that when they were in bed. It is at such seminal moments that I realised this wasn't just my dad; this was a man just like me who had found his love fifty eight years ago, spent a lifetime together and was now close to losing her and feeling so alone in the world. On one of the later visits dad brought his prayer book in and before he left he recited the "*Shema*" – in the Jewish religion it is customary to recite this with/for a person when they are close to death (it is a prayer in praise of god). It is one of the most heart breaking things I have ever experienced. Watching him accepting the inevitable and effectively saying goodbye to the love of his life turned my stomach in knots – I was desperately fighting back the tears (for his sake) and looking across the room I saw Jacqueline was doing the same. I was amazed at the strength of character of dad being able to get through such an ordeal. If I had tried to recite it I would have been in pieces!

As I wheeled dad out of the room I am sure he believed that was the last time he would see Fay. In fact he came in one more time – on Friday 9th June. That date was particularly special as it was their fifty eighth wedding anniversary. For the last few days Jacqueline and I had been desperately hoping that mum did not pass away on this day – it would be such a cruel twist if that happened. Obviously it was very much a bitter/sweet day. The one thing that sticks vividly in my mind was that dad brought in an anniversary card for mum and read it out to her. The words are still burned in my memory as they encapsulated the extreme love and pain dad was experiencing – the card simply read *"To Fay, wherever you are I will always love you, Ian x"*.

As we were getting close to the end, Jacqueline and I had decided that one of us would always be with mum at the hospital, so for the last two or three days we "rotated" a twenty four hour vigil. We were determined that she would not be alone when the final passing came. I found that those times gave some pause for reflection on what was happening/about to happen. The memories are strongest regarding the night times; sitting in the room by the bed in a high backed wing chair trying to get comfortable and feeling the slight breeze coming through a narrowly opened window from the quiet balmy June night. At times there actually seemed to be a real peace surrounding us – almost the calm in the eye of the storm. However, over this time the impending reality was brought home quite starkly as mum's legs etc., started to change colour to a blueish/grey. This was the body making its last efforts to remain alive by channelling the remaining blood and energy to the key organs rather than the extremities.

On Saturday 10th June 2006 I was at the hospital until early afternoon and then Jacqueline arrived to take over (sometime around 2 to 3 p.m.). I left the hospital around 3 p.m. and was driving home when my mobile went about halfway through the fifteen to twenty minute journey. I pulled over to answer it and it was Jacqueline – my heart sank. The first words were so simple yet so devastating – *"she's gone"*. I turned around and headed back to the hospital. I don't think anyone can really be ready for what faced me on entering the room again – the dead body of my wonderful mother; I now only had one parent left in my life.

Jacqueline and I held each other and cried – she said that she looked away to a nurse that had come into the room and when she looked back mum had slipped away. Time almost seemed to stand still for a while. We spent a little time just sitting there, trying to come to terms with what had just happened. After a while we let the nurses know that they could come in and prepare the body for removal to the hospital mortuary. Jacqueline and I agreed that she would go home and break the news to dad while I stayed on and oversaw everything at the hospital. Moira, our neighbour from across the road from the flat, would then come and pick me up when I was ready.

Once Jacqueline had left one of the most striking events happened. The nurses were preparing the body and I was sat in a chair at the right side of the bed, when mum's head rolled to my side and one eyelid was open. Suddenly I looked into this lifeless eye, that had always been so full of love for all of us, and realised I was looking at a shell – not the person that had given me life and brought me into the world. That image burned into my memory. It has taken a long time to dim the image and come to terms with it.

I was asked by the staff if there was any religious person associated with the hospital that they could call to be with me until the move down to the mortuary took place. Obviously, being a Saturday there would be nobody of our faith available (as it was our Sabbath), but I was so desperate for some related support during this time that they contacted a chaplain who came up to keep me company. Eventually staff came and placed mum's body into a large black zipped body bag and lowered it into a trolley type of container. The chaplain and I walked along with the staff as we worked our way down to the mortuary. Just prior to taking the trolley in they asked me if there was any prayer I wanted to say. I wanted to say something but wasn't sure what I should recite at this time (never having faced this situation). Also, I didn't have a Hebrew prayer book with me and certainly could not remember the prayers off by heart. I felt so helpless and awful as I desperately wanted to do everything right for mum – it was the least she deserved. In the end I could remember the first part of the "*Shema*" and so recited that. Then the doors opened to the mortuary, the staff took the trolley inside and I had seen mum for the last time!

I called home to let Jacqueline know I was ready to be picked up and slowly made my way to the entrance/ pick up point. It was a lovely summer's day – yet I have never known the world feel so cold and empty; it had changed irreparably forever. After a few minutes Moira pulled up and I got in. I said to her "she's gone" and then dissolved into sobbing as the realisation of this horrendous loss truly hit me.

Chapter 2

When I got home and walked into the flat dad was sat in his normal chair with his back to the door. I walked round to him, put my arms around him and hugged him. I think Jacqueline joined in as well. I can't remember exactly what I said – I think it was something simple/stupid like "*I'm so sorry*". The three of us holding each other there was I suppose some subconscious attempt to close the circle that had been broken by mum's passing. Although I was in pain I would have done anything at that point to be able to have taken away the grief that dad must have been experiencing. The only crumb of comfort that I had was that he had only seen mum when she was alive – at least he would not have to carry the memories of seeing her dead body with him for the rest of his life.

The immediate task was to contact the synagogue and undertaker to advise them of the situation and to understand what happens next – what things we needed to do and when. Looking back I think part of the fear when you have to deal with a loved one passing, for the first time, is that of the unknown. In the middle of all the grief you realise that you don't know exactly what to do – what happens about death certificates, how do you register the death, what happens in terms of funeral arrangements and moving the body etc. The situation was exacerbated somewhat by the fact that it was the Sabbath and therefore we would not be able to talk to key people in the process until at least the next day. I left messages on the various answerphones and had to wait until Sunday morning for them to call back. I also rang Linda to let her know the news so we could arrange for her to come up to Leeds straight away for the funeral.

On Sunday the undertaker rang back and took me through the various steps that would happen. There was not much he could do until Monday morning, but he would then contact the hospital and confirm an appointment for me to go and pick up the medical death certificate and also ring the Registrar's Office in Leeds to fix an appointment for me to take the medical certificate there and register the death. As part of that registration I would receive a green form which I would pass on to him – this was the authorisation to proceed with the burial and allow him to collect the body from the hospital and proceed with all the required preparations. He also imparted a good practical piece of advice – which I now pass on. He suggested at the time of registering the death I ask for an additional four of five certified copies of the death certificate, as I would need to send these as proof to various organisations e.g. banks/building societies, pension providers etc., when dealing with probate/mum's estate. The cost at that time would only be about £5 each, whereas I would otherwise have to make another appointment in the future with possibly a higher cost involved. In the meantime, over the weekend, Jacqueline and I were also busy contacting family and friends to let them know what had happened and that the funeral would probably be Monday or Tuesday that coming week.

On Monday morning I received the call about the appointments (both arranged for that morning) and set off accordingly. Linda had arrived in Leeds and came with me to provide company and moral support – greatly appreciated and needed. Once all the formalities had been taken care of and I took the green form to the undertaker, he confirmed that the funeral would be later that afternoon.

The speed of arranging the funeral may seem unusual to some people, but the tradition in the Jewish religion is that the funeral should normally take place in the 24/48 hours following the death. The reason is probably due to the fact that in ancient times most people would have been living in the region we now call the Middle East and with the associated heat etc., the quick burial was the most hygienic approach to the situation. However, in modern times it does come with its own challenges in trying to make arrangements, people getting time off work at short notice and coming from a distance.

The formal car came to pick us up later that day. There were five of us – dad, Jacqueline and I and our other halves (Linda and Andreas). We were to make the short journey (just a few minutes) to the synagogue on Street Lane where we would meet up with the hearse. Some friends and family joined us in their own cars from the start; some at the synagogue, whilst others would go straight to the cemetery on Gelderd Road near Gildersome. We drove into the grounds of the syn-agogue, pulled up behind the hearse and got out. I had been holding things together reasonably well until that point, but the sight of the coffin was too much and I broke down in tears. Logic says that having seen the dead body of mum a couple of days earlier and come through that I should have been able to hold things together at the sight of the coffin – but not so. I was to learn in the months and years ahead that there is no real logic to what might trigger a strong emotional reaction to mum's (and subsequently dad's) death. Certain situations or items just have that effect – a very individual matter.

We went into the synagogue where a couple of people were waiting for us. They carried out a ritual which I had been made aware of by the undertaker. They cut a piece of your clothing (the breast pocket of my shirt in my case) and said a particular prayer. The cut item of clothing is symbolic in representing the pain/loss just suffered. They say that although a cut will heal over time the scar will always remain. We then got back into the car and followed the hearse in procession to the cemetery. We went through the centre of Leeds and at one point passed the old Yorkshire Post building, something I had done hundreds of times in my life. I remember looking at it and also all the traffic around us and reflected that for most people this was just another normal day. They would finish their work and go home to their families as they did every day. But we seemed to be in a bubble in the middle of all this normality – except that all there was within the bubble was pain (looking back it seems a very surreal experience).

At the cemetery the coffin was taken into a small building where prayers were said in Hebrew and then a short address was made by the person officiating to talk about mum's life. After that we made our way out into the cemetery following the coffin. I was pushing dad as he was in his wheelchair and all the congregation followed. At the graveside there were further prayers and then the coffin was slowly lowered into the ground. It seemed to me that the level of pain I felt inside kept increasing as the coffin went lower into this awful gaping hole in the ground. It is a tradition that the immediate family (followed by the rest of the family and friends) then use a spade to fill in the earth on top of the coffin until it is fully covered (each person takes two or three shovels full). Throughout all of this I tried not to look at dad or Jacqueline that often as I could see the anguish written all over their faces. I was trying to be strong, but couldn't help the tears flowing as we said the prayers and proceeded through this inevitable ending. Most of the people there gradually dispersed from the graveside, making their way back up the cemetery, leaving just the five of us and my cousins around. One part of me didn't want to leave as it would seal the final goodbye whilst another part was desperate to remove myself from the theatre of pain I was in. Eventually we made our way back to the car and slowly made our silent way home – without mum.

The custom (called "*sitting shiva*") is that for the week following the funeral there are short prayers (about half an hour) held at the family's house each evening when people can come and pay their respects – usually headed up by a rabbi or senior person from the synagogue. After the prayers, people often stay on to chat with the family in a more relaxed atmosphere. During that week a special memorial candle is lit which actually burns for a full seven days before going out. The undertaker had arranged for the prayer books and "low" chairs to be delivered to the flat (the chairs are used by the immediate family).

That Monday night was the first night of prayers. This brought to the surface again the fear of "not knowing" that I mentioned earlier when I was with mum's body at the hospital. There is part of the service where just the immediate family recite a particular prayer ("*Kaddish*") in Hebrew. Always having been the "black sheep" of the family (as Jacqueline would say) I didn't observe a lot of the religious aspects and although I could read Hebrew it was often slow and ponderous when faced with unfamiliar words or sentences. I desperately wanted to do things properly in mum's memory but struggled through those first few nights (with a bit of help/prompting from my cousin) until the prayer became more familiar and fluent. It certainly added to the stress levels at an already highly stressful time!

One night in particular stands out in my memory. There was a man from the synagogue called David Apfel who took the prayers and had a wonderful singing voice. At a particular point he sang a passage in such a deeply sad, soulful way that it brought us to tears. It seemed to encapsulate everything that had happened and the depth of loss we were all feeling – a wonderful moment, but one that made your stomach physically hurt from the grief.

The week ahead was an unusual time. During the days everything was very sombre as you would expect. Apart from dad having to attend his regular dialysis sessions on Tuesday, Thursday and Saturday there was plenty of time to sit and reflect – what we had lost and what was ahead of us. Linda and Andreas had returned home, so it was time for the three of us to start the long healing process.

I must pause at this time to mention the unstinting support from Linda – something that wouldn't change over the years ahead. Throughout the last few months her love and support had been a real crutch in an ever worsening situation. From a practical point of view she took whatever weight off me that she could. Anything that I wanted/needed doing at home she would deal with, so that I could concentrate one hundred percent on the problems in Leeds. And at no time was there any reference to her, her feelings or her needs. It must have been quite lonely at home without me for so much of the time, but never was a single word ever said in that respect. She was intending to come back up to Leeds the weekend after the funeral but I asked her not to and she accepted that without argument. I explained that, at this time, what we really needed was just dad, Jacqueline and I having time alone together in the flat to start to come to terms with what had happened (and she under-stood and respected that). There are moments in life where all you need is some space and the close blood relatives around you that understand and feel the way you do inside without having to talk about it. Having that level of understanding and unquestioning support from my other half was invaluable during these dark times and I thank her from the bottom of my heart.

Looking back over such times it would have helped if I had had access to an easy reference guide, as to what happens in such circumstances and why (particularly from the religious rather than secular/legal aspects). Fortunately, when I was next to be faced with same situation (with dad) I would have the benefit of both practical experience and an exceptionally good book loaned to us by David Gelman (Moira's husband) entitled *"The Jewish Way in Death and Mourning"* by Maurice Lamm.

At the end of the week of *"shiva"* it felt a little like that famous Churchillian saying – *"Now this is not the end; it is not even the beginning of the end; but it is, perhaps, the end of the beginning"*.

There were now some key matters to progress over the coming months. The first was getting care support for dad (in addition to Jacqueline and I); the second was to progress the creation of a fistula for dad; the third was arranging to move him down south and then clear/sell the flat in Leeds and last, but not least, was dealing with the probate regarding mum's passing.

In terms of care support, we had already been in discussions with the private healthcare provider Yorkshire Care – part of the Allied Healthcare group. A very helpful and empathetic gentleman called Howard had come to the flat and gone through our needs and what they could supply. The plan we decided on was that Jacqueline and I would alternate long weekends in Leeds, arriving Friday evening and going back on Tuesday once dad had left for dialysis that day. In between (from Tuesday tea time, when dad returned from dialysis, to Friday evening) there would be a live in care person who would do everything needed – make meals, do the washing and ironing, help dad get up/get ready for bed each day etc. When Jacqueline and I were there we would tend to do the food shopping and any other errands on the Saturday afternoon when dad was out at dialysis. The start of this change was a bit rocky when one of the care workers decided (for personal reasons) to move away shortly after the arrangements had started! However, we then settled down with two ladies – Jocelyn and Mercy – who dad seemed to get on reasonably with. They alternated weeks. We were fortunate that the flat had a single bedroom as well as mum and dad's double, so the carer could be accommodated without a problem. If Jacqueline or I overlapped at all the settee in the living room was reasonably comfortable (and long enough to accommodate me)! There were to be some changes in personnel over the coming months up to the move down south (which took place at the start of December), but dad was amazingly adaptive considering the radical changes that had occurred in his life.

Later in June there was progress on the medical side when they went ahead with the procedure to create a fistula in dad's left forearm. The operation took place at Leeds General Infirmary and went well, but there was (at least) a six week waiting time thereafter before they could attempt to use it for dialysis as it needed to heal and build up strength – so it was a case of wait and see.

On the move front we discussed the options with dad. Both Jacqueline and I lived near each other, with Linda and I having the larger property (three bedroom semi with an en-suite as well as a bathroom, through living/dining room etc.; Jacqueline had a smaller three bedroom mid terrace property with one large living/dining room). Initially dad agreed to move in with Linda and I. As it transpired he would change his mind over the summer and eventually move in with Jacqueline and Andreas. In hindsight I think it proved to be the best approach as things worked out. We started to think about going through everything at the flat (over time – as with dad's state of health this was obviously going to take some weeks or months) to see what he would want to keep/move, sell or dispose of – the thought was quite daunting, as like most couples there would be an extensive array of things to go through after a life-time together, including items in the loft and (my main concern) a garage full of dad's items from over the years (definitely his "man cave"). We also started to have contact with estate agents to get a valuation of the property ready for when it went on the market. We were somewhat restricted in progressing the sale at this stage as we did not know when dad would be able to be transferred to a hospital around Surrey. That would probably entail the fistula being proved as successful and working well as well as finding a dialysis slot at a hospital around Surrey and the consultants agreeing a transfer.

I took on the mantle of dealing with the paper-work regarding mum's probate on behalf of dad. As we already had a power of attorney in place regarding dad this made matters easier. Despite the fact that she had made a hand written note of her wishes, this was never signed and witnessed as a legal document – hence, offi-cially mum died intestate. I give a big thanks to Paul Jacobson at this point. Paul (one of the neighbours from across the road in the cul-de-sac) was a practicing solici-tor and took me through everything required step-by-step, arranging all the paperwork and submissions (including Inheritance Tax Forms). It would still take until early November before the final "letter of adminis-tration" was issued by the district registrar giving me the official power to finalise all of mum's affairs.

In the early weeks though there was still a number of immediate actions to be taken – a whole list of people to notify of Fay's passing (usually needing sight of one of the certified death certificates I had obtained on registering the death) – everything from the pensions people, to banks and building societies, the council (regarding Council Tax amounts/alleviation), return of the Blue Parking Badge etc.

Before I move on, I must just return to Paul Jacobson. He not only was a great help practically regarding mum's probate etc., but he was extremely supportive emotionally. Having lost parents himself he understood the emotional pain and turmoil I was going through (and from a male perspective) and we had many conversations when I dropped over there to progress matters which helped in my coping and coming to terms with what had happened.

One other matter had been on my mind for some time – that of Linda and I. As I have mentioned previously, we met in 1992 and since the mid-nineties had lived together. We had not married for a few reasons – we were both happy together; neither of us were bothered about starting a family and we were not of the same faith. The latter point was not really an issue for either of us, but despite mum and dad and her getting on fine I wasn't quite sure how they would feel about the finality of a marriage (knowing they would not have grandchildren and the fact that both children had married out of the faith – as I was obviously cognisant of their feelings when Jacqueline had married Andreas (Greek Orthodox) in the early nineties). The awful truth was that I could not now discuss the matter with both of them, but I decided to sit down one weekend and talk about dad's feelings on the subject. I took him through my churnings and said that at some time I intended to ask Linda to marry me, but having lost mum I would prefer at least to have him see me get married rather than have two empty chairs at the top table if I carried on waiting. He was quite clear. He asked me if I really loved her and I said yes emphatically. *"Then I suggest you ask her"* were his words. He gave me his support and blessing.

Later in July, when things had settled down more into a routine I decided to take a four day break to crash out and try and recharge the physical and mental batteries. Linda and I had already arranged to have a break in Muscat, Oman back in March before everything blew up, so it seemed easiest to resurrect those plans and arrangements. We arranged it over one of the weekends Jacqueline was in Leeds with dad. We stayed at the Grand Hyatt in Muscat and I called back each evening to ensure there were no major problems (particularly on dialysis days). We had been to the Gulf area many times in the past, but not at that time of the year – it was so hot (hitting a high of around forty degrees centigrade most days) that when we walked out of the hotel to the swimming pool after breakfast on a morning our sunglasses steamed up!! However, it afforded us the opportunity to crash out on a sun lounger in the shade most of the day (just dragging ourselves into the pool – about five yards away – at regular intervals when the heat became unbearable).

One evening I had booked a table at a restaurant in The Chedi hotel for dinner. It had a wonderful setting looking out over a private beach and the sea, with a lovely peaceful setting when wandering through its gardens and pool area. We went over to the hotel a little early and went for a stroll in the garden/pool area before dinner – when I finally popped the question (after fourteen years). Tears ensued (mainly Linda's, rather than mine) and a "yes" (it would have been rather embarrassing after so long had she said no). I felt more at peace the rest of that evening, not only because we were to be married at last, but because (hopefully) dad would be there to share in it.

Chapter 3

I suppose the period up to December 2015 could be classified as *"planning for the new future"*.

On the medical side the fistula seemed to be building up well. Dad had to do an exercise a number of times each day – repeatedly squeezing a soft rubber ball in the palm of his hand – to build up the strength of the new connection. Eventually in late August the hospital decided to try and use the new approach on dad. That entailed putting two fine needles directly into the vein in the forearm for each dialysis session, rather than connecting up to the tubes from his neck. Generally the dialysis went reasonably well, albeit there was always the odd glitch/issue from time to time (as we found from experience in the years ahead). However, it was a further few weeks before they agreed to reverse the procedure in the neck and remove the lines they had inserted there some months ago. They had to be sure the fistula (and dialysis using it) was robust before removing the old lines. For once there was something (relatively) positive for dad – as it was far more comfortable not having the neck lines in and also he could wash/shower without any problems.

Unfortunately, there were still opportunities for health problems to surface as I found one Saturday

morning in Leeds. When dad got up he wasn't at all well – couldn't really eat his breakfast properly and was being sick from time to time. He was still in his dressing gown and it looked unlikely that he would be in a fit state to go in for dialysis. Considering the essential nature of having regular dialysis this could have developed into a major problem. I rang the unit at the hospital and discussed the situation. They were very supportive and helpful. Basically, if we could get dad into the unit (in whatever state) they would look after him i.e. holistically, not just for the dialysis. We eventually managed to get him into a wheelchair and the unit were as good as their word. They gave him an injection to stop the sickness, used a side room so he had privacy and eventually, when he stabilised (some time later), proceeded with the normal dialysis. The one thing that this episode impressed on me was just how dependent and essential the regular dialysis sessions were – on occasions, especially in future winters when snow arrived, this imperative would provide a challenge and high level of stress in terms of physically trying to make the journey to the dialysis centre.

Come the autumn, dad's stability on dialysis meant that his renal doctor (Dr Newstead) was in a position to start to pursue a transfer to a hospital near to where Jacqueline and I lived in Surrey. Unfortunately, our local (excellent) hospital – Frimley Park NHS Foundation Trust – was not a renal centre with regular dialysis. Instead, the nearest hospital was an hour away – Epsom and St Helier's! Dr Newstead wrote to his counterpart at St Helier's in October and eventually a place was secured for dad under Dr Kwan's renal team there. He would attend for an outpatient appointment on

4th December 2006 for the first time and immediately after that continue with his first dialysis session. We now had a firm date and focus for the move (frighteningly short in reality).

In terms of the flat in Leeds, this had now been placed on the market. What we hoped would be a relatively easy sale (as far as any house sale is) proved far from that. We ended up having to switch estate agents during the process and endure three accepted offers that each eventually fell through for various reasons. It would finally be April 2008 before the sale was completed!!

We had already started to sort through various things in the flat each time Jacqueline or I were there. Jacqueline eventually took on the unenviable, and extremely emotional, task of sorting through mum's clothes and belongings and (with dad's consent) gave most of the clothes to the Leeds Jewish Welfare Board who support and help people in need. The one thing she did keep was the nightdress mum was wearing when she passed away in hospital. Dad also accepted that he would have to part with a lot of his prized possessions from the past. As an example, he had a range of woodworking instruments (woodworking planes etc.) that went back to when he was a professional furniture maker in his early days after university. Fortunately, we obtained a contact at one of the technical colleges in Leeds who came over to the flat one day and arranged to sell most of the instruments to students and other people at the college – he even bought one particular item himself, as he said it was far too good to be used by students. We were pleased for dad in this respect, as at least he felt that the items were valued and had gone to good homes – people who would use them and benefit from them.

A sad episode in this vein was having to sort out everything in the garage attached to the flat. It took two or three sessions as there were so many items in there. I would take a chair down from the flat so dad could sit there and then I would start to go through everything, item by item, to see whether he wanted to take it with him, try and sell it, or agree to it being taken away as part of a final "clearance". It must have been quite painful emotionally for dad, as a whole lifetime of items collected (each with their own story or particular significance) needed to be relinquished. At times I had to play devil's advocate pushing him as to, realistically, whether he would ever need or use a particular item again (I was cognisant we would have far less storage space available in Surrey).

I became aware of just how upsetting this proved to be for dad when one day he was getting washed in the bathroom upstairs in the flat. We were chatting and he suddenly mentioned a particular item about which he had changed his mind – and wanted to keep. He described it to me (a board that could be used by architects for drawing plans). I went down to the garage and brought up what I thought was the item – there were two or three similar items in various places in the garage. He said that wasn't the one and gave me a further description. Back down to the garage I went and tried again, bringing up a second board. Again I was told that wasn't what he was talking about. For one of only a few times I got a bit short with dad, probably due to the general strain of everything that was going on and the exasperation of this situation (having thought we had finally dealt with everything in the garage). He had just come out of the bathroom. He looked at me, turned to face the wall of the hallway, put his forearm against the wall at head height, rested his forehead on it and started to cry ... and all he said in a broken voice was "don't shout at me Russell, I've lost everything."

At that moment I wished the ground would have opened up and swallowed me. I felt so terrible and the reality for dad really hit home again. Some months ago he had a fairly normal life – a devoted wife, a warm and comfortable flat, all his possessions acquired over the years, his independence (including driving, shopping etc.) and a passable level of health. As he had just said – that was all gone, or about to disappear, plus he would also be having to leave the city where he had spent most of his life and be linked to dialysis virtually every other day for the rest of his life. I suddenly couldn't comprehend how he was actually managing to cope with what had/was happening. I walked down the hall, put my arms around him and said "dad, don't cry – I'm so, so sorry". I tried to explain that it was just stress/frustration on my part, but I now appreciate that was nothing compared with what he was going through.

We did arrange someone to come with a skip and gradually clear out the garage of everything that was to go – not a pleasant day for dad (it just confirmed the finality of what we were doing).

In Surrey we were also having to make adjustments and plans to accommodate the move. Whenever such situations arise you have to think carefully about all the changes that will be required to accommodate an elderly person with various limitations – sometimes it's the minutia that can trip you up and cause the most problems. As dad had indicated initially he would be moving in with Linda and I, we were making various arrangements. Our front path had two steps at intervals leading up to the house and also a large bush just where you would turn towards the front door. Obviously, we needed to consider the ease of access and especially if we were to need to use a wheelchair for that. Hence, I had been in touch with one of the tradesmen I had used before and he arranged to take out the steps and make the path a gradual incline, as well as removing the bush and putting in paving that would allow easy wheelchair access and turning. We also anticipated the need for additional wardrobe space, so we ending up having a triple wardrobe delivered, which was assembled in the third bedroom (we used it mainly as an office rather than a normal bedroom). The other major task was running power into our garage with a view to getting a large upright freezer installed, so we would have enough space for the extra food we might need – at that time we just had a small (half) freezer in the kitchen.

However, over the summer dad asked me if I would be upset if he changed his mind and moved in with Jacqueline. I said it was not a problem and that he should go where he wanted to – as we only lived a few minutes away from each other, distance from one sibling to the other wasn't going to be an issue. So similarly Jacqueline then started to make arrangements and changes that would accommodate dad. One of the major changes was the need to install a stair lift to get up and down stairs. Mum and dad had one installed on the communal stairs in the flat in Leeds (with the flat being on the first floor), but fortunately that was a straight staircase. Jacqueline would need to have one installed that went around corners as her staircase was rounded at the top and bottom. It proved to be a bit of a challenge due to a relatively narrow hallway at the bottom (necessitating a hinged arm on the main rail) and the need to adjust the steps at the top (so there was somewhere flat for dad to step onto when he got off the stair lift). It also shocked us as to how expensive such items can prove to be!

The other aspect, which is not immediately obvious, is the need to transfer to a new doctor, dentist, chiropodist etc. Generally you would not think that was a major challenge, but considering dad's mobility issues we needed to track down a dentist that had at least one room/surgery on the ground floor so there was easy wheelchair access – not that easy, as Jacqueline was to find out. We were fortunate in that she also found a chiropodist that would carry out home visits, so that made life easier. These are the sort of challenges that most people who are able bodied never consider (and why should they), but are crucial when looking after someone who has such restrictions.

Back in Leeds there were a couple of changes that Yorkshire Care had to make over the months leading up to dad's move. One of the original ladies had been pregnant when she started looking after Ian and eventually had to stop work to have the baby. Another changed work, so there were a couple of alternative carers that were brought in over time. Unfortunately, they probably didn't gel as well with dad as the original people, but they saw us through to the move in December. Also Moira (from across the road from the flat) provided some support during these months. She used to do dressmaking from home and often would pop over and keep dad company whilst still carrying on with some of her work – I think in hindsight this contact with what life was like before the events of this year was helpful for dad and the friendship would remain throughout the rest of his life.

It's interesting to reflect on some of the changes that ensue when you lose someone close. I had always been heavily into music ever since I was in my early teens. The first thing I would do when I got in my car would be to put on music/put in a CD etc. Albeit not consciously, I suddenly realised that ever since mum had passed away I hadn't listened to music in the car. I would sometimes put on a news station on the radio, but that was all. It wasn't a conscious decision, but just something that felt right (it would somehow have felt wrong to be listening to music). It would take the best part of a couple of years for that situation to revert back to what it was – and even today I do not sing along to music to the extent I used to. I found I could easily drive the three to four hours journey home from Leeds and not have the entertainment system on in the car.

Another more obvious change is that of emotions surfacing. Obviously, there were many tears shed in the initial weeks and months. There are still times today when something suddenly triggers the sadness and tears well up again. One thing I find interesting is that sometimes it is not the obvious things that sets this off – I could drive home from Leeds, walk in our front door and then suddenly dissolve into tears (much to Linda's concern initially). Even today there are odd instances that still evoke such a reaction. I remember watching a re-run episode of the television series Boston Legal the other week. In it one of the partners of the legal firm featured found herself at a hospital with her father suffering and dying – she was faced with the decision of whether or not to turn off the life support machine. At that point she was sat at the bedside holding her father's hand – I got up off the settee and said to Linda "I can't watch the rest of this" and stepped out of the room. All of a sudden, after a number of years, the mirrored pain of sitting with mum (and subsequently dad) as they were close to death came flooding back. Although you come to live with the losses of those close to you, the painful memories are often not far below the surface even years after the event.

A similar trigger, for me, exists in the words of one of the tracks of a favourite rock group – Pink Floyd. Every time I hear this, or listen to it being performed by one of the tribute bands, like The Australian Pink Floyd, it brings me to tears. The key line is ... "*hanging on in quiet desperation is the English way, the time is gone, the song is over, thought I'd something more to say*". It's from the track Time on the classic album Dark Side of the Moon. To me it encapsulates probably what we will all feel at the time of reckoning – that life has gone so quickly and that there's still so much we want to do or say. It is particularly poignant in mum and dad's cases where their endings were not quick, but a prolonged slide to death (particularly in dad's case as will be revealed later). It never ceases to amaze me how such young men (as Pink Floyd were when they wrote this back in 1973) could write such an insightful line about age and death.

The above are just some of the examples of how the loss of a parent has affected me. I am sure Jacqueline has many of her own examples that she could add. This is another example of where we are all intensely individual in the things that affect us regarding bereavement, yet from the other perspective it is something that universally we all experience and with which we have to cope.

Over the summer and autumn we also turned our minds to the gravestone that we would have erected for mum. Although the consecration (stone setting ceremony) would not be until late spring/early summer the following year we ideally needed to agree the wording and place the order for the stone before dad left Leeds. As the stone would be imported it would take a few months for it to arrive after ordering and then there was the lettering to engrave and other matters to finalise. After discussing it with dad we agreed on a double headstone as he had reserved his burial plot next to mum at the time of the funeral. Also at that time Jacqueline and I had reserved the plots on either side of mum and dad's at the cemetery, so eventually we all would be re-united as a family – in a fashion. The stone would be black granite with gold lettering thereon. In the Jewish religion the wording on the headstones normally follow a very similar pattern. There are names and details in Hebrew at the top and we agreed for mum the rest of the wording would read:

"TREASURED MEMORIES OF A
DARLING WIFE AND DEVOTED MOTHER
FAY HARRIS
PASSED AWAY 10th JUNE 2006
AGED 91 YEARS

DEEPLY MOURNED AND SADLY MISSED BY
HER BELOVED HUSBAND IAN,
ADORING CHILDREN JACQUELINE AND RUSSELL,
SON-IN-LAW, FAMILY AND FRIENDS

SHALOM".

Although it was necessary to agree these details well in advance of the actual consecration it certainly wasn't made any easier by the recency of the loss – the stark reminder staring up at you from the wording on the draft page we had to agree and sign-off.

Jacqueline and I were continuing with our alternating long weekends in Leeds. We would usually fly up from Heathrow to Leeds Bradford Airport on British Midland, as it was quicker and easier than driving up – plus we had the benefit of extremely cheap staff travel interline fares (one of the big benefits of working for an airline). We would get a taxi from the airport to the flat in Leeds, as it was only about fifteen minutes away, and then use dad's car as necessary when we were there. One Tuesday on a return flight I had my legs crossed in my seat. As I uncrossed them, in the limited space between seats, I felt something in my right knee "tweak". At the time I didn't think too much about it but in the following days I started to fear that I had torn part of the cartilage. The reason I suspected that, was due to the fact that I had badly torn a cartilage back in my school days when I was doing rugby training and despite the years I could still remember the sorts of feelings that were associated with it. I arranged to see a specialist fairly quickly who scanned the knee and confirmed my fear. They say timing is everything and I did think "sod's law", just when I need to be fit to deal with everything in Leeds and the move this should suddenly happen (after a gap of nearly forty years) – but life is sometimes like that.

When I had undergone the knee operation as a teenager it had been quite extensive, entailing a week's stay in hospital and many weeks bandaged up from thigh to ankle. Fortunately, the advances of medical science in those forty years meant that the prognosis this time was radically different. The doctor confirmed that they could do keyhole surgery to trim off the torn piece of cartilage and that I would be in and out of hospital the same day!! He said that I would need physiotherapy for a few weeks afterwards, but would be driving and walking around reasonably within a couple of weeks.

Based on the fact that we would be moving dad down to Surrey at the beginning of December, I arranged for the operation mid-October so I would be in a reasonable state to help with the arrangements and the move. I actually returned from one of the weekends in Leeds on Tuesday 17th October and was in BMI Runneymede Hospital at seven o'clock the following morning. Amazingly, just as the doctor had said, I (gingerly) walked out of the hospital that same day when Linda came in to pick me up around four o'clock. By the next time I was due to go up to Leeds (Friday 27th October) I was in a reasonable state.

A little later (around mid-November) we finally got the Letters of Administration through for mum's probate. At last I could tie up a lot of the loose ends on behalf of dad. This meant closing down certain savings accounts and transferring the money to dad's account. Also we confirmed to organisations where they had held joint accounts that they should now be held just in dad's name. Despite the fact that mum had died intestate we followed her written wishes in passing on certain personal effects to Jacqueline and I. This enabled part of the "closure" that people talk about to take place.

As the date of the move came closer we made arrangements with Pickfords moving company to carry out the necessary packing and transfers. The logistics were somewhat complex. From discussions with dad we had all agreed that some furniture and boxes would accompany him to Jacqueline's house, other furniture and boxes would come to my place and a third category would go into storage (which we would gradually sort out over time). We also had to fit this in around dad's dialysis sessions (the last one in Leeds and the first one at St Helier's) and physically bringing him down to Surrey by car – good game!

Pickfords came and did most of the packing on Saturday 2nd December, albeit the first delivery at Jacqueline's place would not be until after lunch on the Monday. It was a difficult time for all of us emotionally, but particularly for dad – he was leaving his home, where he had spent so many happy years with mum, and the city he had lived in since World War II for a completely new life. Although he would see the neighbours again on future visits back to Leeds, the goodbyes were a difficult time. I drove him down in my car and Jacqueline drove dad's old Fiesta down (it was originally her car some years ago). We would sell that car fairly soon after the move as dad reluctantly agreed that his driving days were now over. When we got down to Surrey we needed to split responsibilities as dad had an outpatients appointment with Dr Kwan at St Helier's at 09:30 a.m. on Monday 4th December and then dialysis from 1:30 p.m. onwards (we had managed to move the days for his dialysis to Monday, Wednesday and Friday from Tuesday, Thursday and Saturday). That same afternoon we were expecting Pickfords to deliver to Bagshot (Jacqueline's home). Jacqueline stayed with dad at the hospital and I agreed to deal with the delivery in Bagshot. The following day Pickfords would then deliver to my house and I would accompany them from there to Access Storage in Camberley, to deposit the remaining items. Referring back to the dialysis days, this change was much better as dad would have a "normal" weekend off every week – a benefit with Jacqueline still working full time.

Initially the dialysis went reasonably. The set up was somewhat different from Leeds with quite a noisy main ward where the dialysis took place and nothing in particular to distract the patients from their session – I seem to remember there was one old TV at the end of the ward which was not easy for people to see. Also it wasn't always the same nurse(s) that would put dad on/ take dad off dialysis each time. This was an important factor as (a) he had finer needles used than the standard ones (they were colour coded green, red etc.) and (b) his blood pressure was lower than most people's, albeit he tolerated the dialysis well (considering the fact that dialysis tends to depress blood pressure over the session and his age). Again, stepping back and trying to be objective for a minute it was understandable given the pressure the NHS was (and still is) under, but as was to be proved later on, when we switched dialysis centres, having a small number of staff who really know the patients and their individual (clinical) peculiarities is highly beneficial.

Going forward the arrangements to get dad to and from St Helier's was by hospital transport. They would pick him up from the house around mid to late morning, but would also pick up a number of other patients from around Surrey. Hence, the journey in could well be around one to one and a half hours – not ideal considering the procedure they were then going to undergo that afternoon – very draining. Even more of a problem was to be the transport home. In theory the system should have worked the same in reverse, but not so. Firstly, dad was on dialysis for three and a half hours each time, but other patients had to have four hour sessions. Hence, there could be quite a lot of waiting around post dialysis until all the relevant patients had come off. Then the route taken to drop off people could vary immensely, so at times dad could almost be the last person to be dropped off – as we were in Surrey Heath, right at the north western edge of Surrey. Hence, although technically dad could finish his dialysis around five o'clock we had a number of occasions when he didn't arrive home until eight o'clock or later!

It rapidly became obvious that the distance and transport situation was not going to be tenable for dad for any length of time (and would contribute to his deterioration). In the short term we made the decision to pick him up after dialysis ourselves – at least he would then not be waiting around and could be whisked home directly in comfort. As Jacqueline's husband, Andreas, was working in Kingston (fairly close by) he agreed to swing by and pick dad up at least one evening a week. I would drive over on another day and Jacqueline would try and get off work a little early to pick him up the third day. At that stage we still let the transport pick him up to take him in, as that was the lesser of the two problems.

The other, fortunate, fact that came to light was that a new satellite dialysis facility was being built at West Byfleet, Surrey – only about twenty minutes away from us. It was to be run by a company called Fresenius, albeit contracted by St Helier's Hospital. There were already another one or two satellite centres within Surrey (and Hampshire), but obviously they had limited capacity and the turnover of patients was very low – hence, trying to get a place in one of those was extremely difficult. The other downside of these satellite centres was that there was no doctor on site – just nurses. Thus, if a more serious medical situation arose they would not be able to deal with it on site (unlike the situation at the main hospital) and would have to call an ambulance etc. Over the coming weeks we talked about the options with dad's renal specialist – Dr Marsh. He was quick to point out the additional risks for dad associated with dialysing at a satellite centre, given his age, condition, angina situation etc. However, he did appreciate that there would be a considerable upside to having the centre so close to home, therefore saving the extensive journeys and impact on dad's health. In the end dad said he was willing to accept the elevated risk and Dr Marsh agreed that, subject to dad's medical condition being stable, he would authorise the transfer to the new centre when it opened around August 2007 – so we had a few more months to ride out the St Helier's situation.

The move to Surrey changed everybody's lives – not just dads'. With Jacqueline working full time at

Heathrow I initially took on the mantle of looking after dad during the weekdays. On dialysis days I would go over in the morning and help him get up/dressed and then do breakfast etc. I would stay until the transport came to pick him up late morning. Then, as mentioned above, one of us would collect him from the hospital at tea time. On Tuesdays and Thursdays I would spend most of the day with dad until Jacqueline came home from work in the evening. At the weekend Linda and I used to drop in most Saturday and Sunday afternoons, so Jacqueline and Andreas could go out shopping together etc. This arrangement stayed in place until we engaged some external help and support around May 2007 (more on this later). It was fortunate that I had taken early retirement from British Airways the previous April, as I now had the capacity to deal with the situation and provide the support necessary.

On a more upbeat note we started to try and settle dad in to his new way of life. One afternoon I took him up to Waterside – British Airways headquarters near Heathrow where Jacqueline now worked (having moved across from the Terminals at Heathrow). It gave him the opportunity to see this new world which Jacqueline and I had talked about so often. Also Jacqueline booked tickets for all of us to go and see a matinee of the pantomime "Cinderella" on 30th December at the New Victoria Theatre (our major, local theatre in Woking). Dad had always enjoyed the theatre (as had mum) and pantomime in particular. Unfortunately, during the last few years of mum's life her mobility problems and acute deafness made trips to the theatre a thing of the past – so it felt good to bring something positive back into dad's life, despite everything with which he was having to cope.

Prior to that though we all had to go through one of a number of "firsts". When you are faced with bereavement, people always say the first year is the hardest. Not just for obvious reasons surrounding the immediacy of the loss, but because so many events that had previously been taken for granted get changed. One of those was Christmas. For every year in my life Christmas had always been at home with mum and dad – whether in the house in Harrogate Road where I was brought up or the flat in Cresta Court. This year would be very different. We had Christmas and Boxing day at Jacqueline's house, but of course I had no presents to buy for mum and when we were about to sit down around the table for Christmas lunch it suddenly hit home hard that there was one person missing – I stood in the doorway looking across to the table with dad sat there and started to cry. I seem to remember Jacqueline putting her arms around me and saying quietly "I know".

Going through such episodes is an inevitability, and future birthdays and wedding anniversaries would elicit a similar response in the months ahead. However, in hindsight it is just one part of that multi- faceted subject of healing after a loss.

Chapter 4

The first half of 2007 proved to be a mix of looking back, a period of change/adjustment and planning for the future.

Back in the second half of 2006 Linda and I had started to plan our wedding. We had managed to obtain a booking at the Manor House Hotel, Newlands Corner in Surrey for Sunday 17th June 2007 at 4 p.m. As anyone will know who has had anything to do with a wedding, booking the venue is just the first of what seems an endless list of matters to arrange – who to invite, table plans, invitations, table centre pieces, flowers, arranging the registrar and vows, speeches, transport, photos etc., etc. Although we discussed and agreed everything jointly, I made most of the arrangements as Linda was still working full time.

Similarly Jacqueline and I were making the arrangements for the consecration of mum's headstone in Leeds. Again, co-ordination was the key element, trying to align a date that worked for us with availability via the synagogue (who arranged someone to officiate) and the availability of a place called Donisthorpe Hall in Leeds where we would lay on refreshments after the ceremony. Donisthorpe was a well-known care home for the elderly in North Leeds (not far from where mum and dad's flat was). Within the building there was a small "implanted" synagogue, at which dad held the position of Life President as recognition for all his extensive work for the synagogue over many years. We intended to unveil a memorial plaque for mum in the synagogue after returning from the cemetery and then proceed with the refreshments in the lounge area of Donisthorpe thereafter. We managed to secure the date of the 10th June 2007 – a year to the day after mum's passing.

Having learned from the issues surrounding mum's probate, I arranged for dad to draw up a Will in January 2007. Linda and I had used a firm called Gibson Forge Associates (now Ash Wills) to draw up our Wills and found them to be excellent. They took all the hard work out of the process by coming out to your home, drawing up the draft documentation and then sending it through to you for final tweaks/approval. They even arranged for the signed version to be stored safely for a small charge. As most items reverted to dad in mum's case the situation of dying intestate was not a big issue, apart from slowing down the granting of probate and therefore officially tying up various loose ends. However, the existence of a Will would be more important where dad was concerned as there would be a split of items between Jacqueline and I. It is very easy to put off such actions as drawing up a Will – after all it brings into focus a person's mortality, which is not a subject most people wish to ponder – but like most matters, if dealt with early, it will make future processes that much smoother (especially beneficial at a time when all involved will be stressed and emotional). Also, you never know what the future may bring and suddenly the person concerned may not have the mental capacity to draw up and sign such a document.

Dad's dialysis was going reasonably (despite the long journeys involved), but there were always glitches/problems from time to time. One in particular was always the chance of a "blow out" which normally occurred when having the needles put in (or by a person moving their dialysis arm if the needles were not securely attached). This results in a needle going *through* a vein rather than *into* it and hence blood leakage both under the skin and externally. Under such situations the dialysis has to be stopped immediately and time given for the vein to repair and the blood/swelling to dissipate. I remember getting a call from the hospital one afternoon to say that such an event had occurred with dad and that they had obviously stopped the dialysis part way through. They indicated I could come and pick him up at any time. I said I would drive over straight away and for them to let dad know I was on my way (albeit it would take nearly an hour to get to St Helier's). When I got there what greeted me really tugged at my emotions. I walked in to the ward and saw dad on his bed curled up in a foetal position. At that moment he looked like a small, sad and vulnerable child. In my eyes my father had always been a tower of strength and a real role model to me in every way – and now to see him reduced to this was very hard for me emotionally. The roles of life had been reversed and it was Jacqueline and I who were looking after and comforting him. I wandered over and put my arm around him and said "come on dad, let's take you home".

It wasn't such one off incidents on their own that were of concern, but the fact that if the blow out was particularly serious it could impede the ability to dialyse using the fistula going forward, which would create urgent, serious problems – it all comes back to the tread-mill of having to dialyse every two to three days, or become ill very quickly. So the fear of damage to the arm/fistula was an ever constant in the background.

The other matter that Jacqueline and I monitored closely was dad's angina episodes. As mentioned previously, he had unstable angina which meant that attacks were not necessarily brought on by exertion – he could be in bed, or sitting in his armchair watching TV and he could start with chest pains. If not dealt with immediately they could (and had in the past) resulted in the need for an ambulance, with all the resulting trauma and issues associated with being taken to hospital. He always kept a little bottle of prescribed GTN (glyceride tri-nitrate) spray in his pocket or on the bedside table. That was to spray under his tongue in the event of an attack. Ideally this would result in the pain subsiding and disappearing within three or four minutes. If not we would repeat the spray. Usually one or two sprays had the desired effect, although there were to be occasions ahead where we did have to call for an ambulance. Jacqueline and I used to keep a close record of these attacks – dates when they occurred, where dad was/what he was doing and how long they lasted/how many sprays were needed. This proved critical in working with his GP and doctors as the frequency (and change thereof) dictated some adjustment of his medication (reducing or increasing the dosage). One of the key things I learned throughout this time was how sensitive people can be to medication. With dad it only necessitated small changes in the dosages of some of his tablets to either stabilise, or de-stabilise, him. Looking back at my diaries he did reasonably well in 2007, as I only recorded six notable episodes. However, as time went by this number would inevitably increase (e.g. ten in 2008; twenty one in 2009 etc.).

One of the positive aspects of monitoring dad's health closely was the ability to access his monthly blood results. Each month they would take blood samples pre and post dialysis. The results were available a few days later and covered a whole range of measures. The hospital gave us access, via the internet, to a site on which we could pick up these results. The site also indicated what each measure was for, the standard range for results and the potential implications of being above/below that range. I actually set up a spreadsheet and copied the results across each month, highlighting in red any items outside the expected range. It was useful so dad could see how he was doing and also proved beneficial whenever he ended up being taken to hospital – as it provided the examining doctors with a quick battery of initial information. Even at home with dad if he didn't feel too great it was a positive approach to be able to say that his standard blood results all looked good that month.

We had tried to retain some contact/continuity with Leeds after the move. There used to be a weekly newspaper (the Jewish Telegraph) which mum and dad bought and Jacqueline arranged a subscription to have it delivered to Bagshot, so dad could still keep in touch with various news. Also, Moira Gelman kept in constant touch with dad. She would usually ring three times a week and catch up on everything (at both ends). She also visited dad a number of times over the years in Surrey. I think this helped with the transition, as he started to feel that all communication had *not* been severed with Leeds and that with the visits we would make to Leeds once or twice a year he had not lost that part of his life completely.

Similarly, I was needing to make regular visits to Leeds to ensure everything was okay with the flat and try to progress the sale. We had left a minimal amount of items in the flat – a single bed in the second bedroom, the three piece suite, hoover and certain items in the kitchen. It was obviously extremely sparse, but allowed me to stay there when I went up. I spent about four weekends there during the first half of 2007, making sure the place was still presentable, dealing with any issues and liaising with the estate agents etc. It was a strange and somewhat unnerving experience. Emotionally it was sad and unsettling as it brought back all the memories of a warm, loving and wonderful home – yet it was now reduced to an empty shell. I have always had a problem believing in an afterlife, but certain nights I would lie in bed in the flat in the complete quiet and wonder whether mum would "appear" to me in some way – now there was nobody else there. I know, in hindsight, it was irrational but I suppose a part of me was still longing for some kind of proof that she had not totally gone (it would have provided an amazing peace of mind and closure). Mind you, if something had appeared I would have probably had a heart attack myself with the shock!!

Back in Surrey we did start to go through some of the boxes and items we had in storage. The only time we were all around was usually the weekends, so there was limited opportunity to go through items, as going through a whole load of pieces in a box and dad deciding if he wanted to keep them, whether Jacqueline and I would like them or whether they should be put on one side to be sold/given to charity, was a slow and painstaking process. Also, it was not a comfortable process for dad – as it obviously surfaced a range of emotions about the loss, move and memories. It would take quite a long time to finally go through the items in storage – we kept moving them to a smaller unit at Access Storage every so often as we managed to get through a number of boxes (I think we moved units about three times).

There were also other times that reminded us of mum during those early months – her birthday in March, Mother's Day etc. Not needing to buy cards and presents was a sobering experience. I sometimes paused for a moment to watch people in card shops buying their cards and presents and wondered if they really appreciated the fact that they had a mum to whom they could give them. I now hadn't a mum to whom I could take them home. Those days always seemed particularly sombre, no matter what we were doing.

Around May 2007 we decided to engage some support in terms of looking after dad on an ongoing basis. We considered various agencies and settled on one nearby. We arranged for someone to come in on dad's non-dialysis days (Tuesday and Thursday) from about eleven o'clock in the morning to three o'clock in the afternoon. After his dialysis days dad was quite drained and did not use to get up until eleven o'clock or later. The support person would help him get ready after getting up, give him breakfast and then would do other housework such as cleaning, washing and ironing in the remainder of the time. I would then ensure that I came round before she went until Jacqueline got home later on in the day. It certainly alleviated some pressure from Jacqueline in terms of the general chores and also allowed me a little more time to deal with other things on Tuesday and Thursday mornings.

Despite the fact that Jacqueline and I put together a comprehensive set of notes on what to do (including precisely what dad had for breakfast and how, how the washing machine worked etc.,) the first person proved an abortive attempt (she had great difficulty even operating the washing machine)! However, we soon got established with another young lady who would be with us for some time. As always, dad was determined to (more than) pay his way and from the time he moved down we set up a standing order to transfer an amount to Jacqueline's bank account each month to cover all additional costs (such as food, care support, additional utility costs etc.). It is certainly a positive step for people in the position dad found himself in to still feel that they are paying their way – it is probably the only element of "independence" that remains in such circumstances. It was ironic (in one respect) that all the sensible saving and fiscal housekeeping exhibited over the years was, in dad's mind, to build up a nest egg to look after mum when he was gone. He said a number of times that considering all his ongoing medical problems he was convinced he would pass away first and he wanted to make sure mum would be financially secure. He never thought for a minute those funds would be supporting him in this situation.

In case the above appears to portray a dour or mundane period, it is worth highlighting that there were positive and enjoyable times as well. We went to the theatre a number of times with dad, seeing such diverse performances as High Society, 42nd Street and the opera Aida. Also, when he felt up to it, we would go out for the odd weekend meal, either locally to the Beefeater or to places like Chez Gerard's in Guildford. Over the summer period we would have afternoons out visiting the gardens at RHS Wisley, stately homes nearby etc. I believe all these activities were extremely beneficial to dad's ongoing health and state of mind. Without such outings it would have been quite easy to fall into the negative spiral of just sitting at home waiting for the next dialysis session and thinking what is the point of this type of life. An even bigger activity was to take place later in the autumn when dad hit the grand age of ninety – but more about that later.

One of the learning points in terms of looking after someone else is that it is equally important to try and look after yourself as well. Keeping healthy in body and mind is key, especially if the period of looking after someone is going to stretch over many months or years. Linda and I had managed a week away in February, going on a Caribbean cruise out of Houston. It was just what was needed to re-charge the batteries after a year of upheaval and stress. Jacqueline also managed a couple of periods away with Andreas – a week around late May and then just under a week at the end of July/early August. Visiting a health club/gym (or taking other regular exercise) also proves to be beneficial (helps clear the mind and relieve some of the stress). Linda and I were already members of a health club over at West Byfleet (very close to where the new satellite dialysis centre was being built) and we tried to get down there a couple of times a week – usually Wednesday evenings to use the gym and I did an advanced Step class on Sunday mornings.

As we moved into June it was time for us all to return to Leeds together for mum's consecration. We had booked the Britannia Hotel out towards Leeds Bradford Airport for the weekend of 9th/10th June, including a disabled room for dad. Although at this point he was still using his sticks to get around the house and very short distances he was having to use a wheelchair for anything else – so the disabled room gave more space and more appropriate bathroom facilities. In advance of going to Leeds I had talked to the person who would officiate at the cemetery and gave them a potted history of mum's life as they would make a short address before the actual consecration took place. We took both cars (Jacqueline's and mine) as not only were there five people but a mountain of luggage/extras to take – including the wheel chair, Zimmer frame, V pillow that dad used in bed and a lot more.

It was a weekend of very mixed emotions for dad. On the up side he was making a return visit to Leeds for the first time since moving down to Surrey at the end of 2006. It would give him the opportunity to see close friends and family and catch up with them all. However, it was also a stark and extremely painful reminder of everything he had lost and no doubt would re-open the wounds that had started to heal over the previous year.

The Saturday was generally a good day, meeting up with people as planned. Sunday morning started with breakfast at the hotel and we packed and checked out at lunchtime. The stone setting was planned for 1.30 p.m. at the cemetery near Gildersome and everyone who was attending met up there in the car park a short time beforehand. Obviously, there was not a coffin as a focal point this time, but there would be a headstone with mum's name on it! There was a short service held in a small building at the entrance to the cemetery. As part of this the person officiating went through a synopsis of mum's life – it was strange and painful to hear such a eulogy. In the past it had always been about someone else's close relative, but this time is was our mother. I generally managed to keep my emotions under control during this part of the service – and then we made our way out onto the cemetery and the long, slow walk down to the graveside. I was pushing dad in his wheel-chair and my mind was flitting between holding my own emotions in check and thinking of how terrible dad must be feeling at this time.

On reaching the graveside there was a sheet covering the headstone. It was then removed to reveal the bold, gold inscription on the black granite stone as we had agreed some months earlier. A further part of the service was carried out and at one point it was down to the immediate family – dad, Jacqueline and I – to recite the prayer of mourning ("*Kaddish*"). The custom was that this was recited each day for the first year after losing a parent, so by now I had become completely familiar with it, unlike at the time of mum's funeral and the immediate period thereafter. However, being able to recite it easily just allowed more of me to dwell on the ongoing loss and again some tears started to trickle down my face.

I think for all of us it felt as if someone had just opened up an old wound again as we stared at this final resting place. As it was a double headstone with a blank left hand side it must have been particularly distressing and chilling for dad – in not many years' time there would be equivalent gold lettering on this, currently, blank side. As the other people attending gradually dispersed and made their way back to the entrance to the cemetery we took a minute or two for reflection at the graveside. The one good thing was that instead of the mound of earth we had left a year ago there was now a fitting memorial for mum. Something to mark the wonderful person she was. There was some element of closure in this respect. I gradually pushed dad back up the cemetery path (still with my eyes welling up with tears) and we made our way out of the cemetery. Even to this day, whenever I visit the cemetery the feeling that I have left something behind always fills me up on departing the grounds.

We made our way back to Donisthorpe Hall in the car for 2.45 p.m. and entered the small implanted synagogue there. A further short ceremony ensued which ended with a small plaque being unveiled with mum's details thereon. It simply said:

In loving memory of

FAY HARRIS

14 Sivan 5766   10 June 2006

Whenever the anniversary of mum's death occurred in future (called *"Yahrzeit"* in the Jewish religion), this plaque would be illuminated in the synagogue and the prayer of mourning recited – this would help to ensure her memory always lived on.

With all the formalities now concluded, everyone retired into the lounge where we arranged for tea, cakes and sandwiches to be served. Out of the whole day this was probably the only pleasant time for dad. It gave time for him to talk to various relatives and friends, catch up and reminisce about times gone by. After a while it was time to start the long drive back to Surrey and for dad to resume the new chapter in his life. It was a fairly quiet trip back, albeit tinged with a certain amount of calmness in the knowledge that everything had been done properly to honour mum in the way she deserved.

The following week was more enjoyable and full of anticipation. The wedding for Linda and I was planned for the following Sunday – 17th June – at 4 p.m. We were both busy making all the final arrangements that week, ensuring everything got to where it should be at the right time (a bit of a logistical challenge). Things started to ramp up on the Friday beforehand. The first event was Hazel and Jim Wilton arriving from Yorkshire, who were going to stay at our house until the wedding. Hazel was one of my oldest friends. We had met decades ago (!) when I was presenting on hospital radio in Leeds in my early twenties. My show was an hour on Friday evenings on Radio Allerton, the hospital radio for Chapel Allerton Hospital near where we lived in North Leeds. One of the presenters also had a programme at the hospital radio station at the Leeds General Infirmary in the centre of Leeds and I had gone down to sit in on the show one evening. Who should be there but Hazel – and the rest, as they say, is history (we have been close friends ever since). I had also known Jim for some years since he and Hazel had got together and I had asked him to be my best man.

Saturday also saw the arrival of Linda's brother Eddie, his son Edward and Linda's mum and dad Joyce and Eddie (confused – you will be)! Linda's parents lived in Taunton, Somerset so Eddie had gone down there and driven them up for the wedding. He would also take them back afterwards. At the same time Chris and Marianne Wilcox arrived from Bermuda. Marianne was the Station Manager for British Airways in Bermuda. I had met her (and Chris) the first time I had visited Bermuda on British Airways business way back in the autumn of 1980. We had immediately hit it off and remain friends to this day – I have been fortunate in visiting Bermuda more times than I can remember over the years (definitely in the teens). On this occasion I had asked Marianne if she would be prepared to give the reading at the wedding ceremony and she said she would love to do that.

We had booked rooms for all these guests at the Holiday Inn in Woking and met up there with everyone that evening for a pre-wedding evening meal we had arranged (Linda's family had actually spent the afternoon with us at the house). Normally this would have been a fairly carefree time, enjoying the company of all the close family and friends around us, but there was a shadow hanging over the proceedings. As we were having all the family guests at our house that afternoon I went over to see dad on the Saturday morning rather than in the afternoon as usual. I got there to find that he wasn't at all well and was still in bed. He was to stay in bed the whole day! We were not sure what the problem was, whether it was just a more extreme effect of a full week's dialysis or whether he had picked up a virus etc. After having got so close I now wondered whether

I would be robbed of having dad at my wedding at the last moment. Potentially the impact would be even greater, as if he remained ill it was likely that Jacqueline would have to stay with him as well – so I could be faced with having neither of them at the wedding. I know dad was determined to be there come hell or high water, but even determination can sometimes only take you so far – we would have to let the clock tick down and see what Sunday brought. They were all due to be at the pre-wedding dinner as well, but that was obviously not an option in the circumstances. This was just another dip in the rollercoaster ride that is set out in this book.

The evening at the Holiday Inn was as enjoyable as possible given the circumstances. I held my breath and rang Jacqueline the following morning. Although dad wasn't particularly good he insisted he would be at the wedding – a sigh of relief (as long as it wouldn't prove too much in the end for him). I won't bore you with the blow by blow details of the wedding, suffice it to say that it went off well and the weather held for us (particularly helpful as we had a lot of outdoor photos to be taken, post ceremony drinks on the patio and in the grounds of the hotel). It was a relatively small affair, with only forty four people attending. The Registrar who performed the ceremony was a lady called Rosie Cooper. She had been a member of cabin crew at British Airways previously – they say it's a small world! Little did we know that we were to meet up with Rosie again a few years later, albeit in more sombre circumstances.

Although dad wasn't great, the opportunity to meet up again with the family from Leeds and a number of friends he knew seemed to buck him up. He always responded well to such social environments and they seemed to have a beneficial effect on him. The day was a double celebration as it also happened to be Father's Day as well!

Even during these happy times mum was never forgotten. An extract from my groom's speech made that clear ".....As many of you are aware, my mother passed away a year ago last week. There isn't a day goes by that she's not in our thoughts (and I'm sure a number of you who knew Fay feel the same) and in some way I *know* she's with us all here today". On a lighter note I did recount an amusing episode that took place in our kitchen in the house on Harrogate Road in Leeds when I was young. Probably like most young boys I was a bit of a handful and I was playing up in the kitchen when my great aunt was there. Mum ended up with her hands around my throat and Auntie Ray said "don't Fay, you'll kill him" to which mum amusingly replied "that's the general idea"! Fortunately there were no ill effects – at least that's my conclusion anyway. It does remind me though of a quote by Neil deGrasse Tyson I came across which was *"we spend the first year of a child's life teaching it to walk and talk and the rest of its life to shut up and sit down"*!

I must admit I thought long and hard about talking about mum in my speech, as I didn't want to put a dampener on the proceedings, but in the end it would have seemed totally wrong not to have included her – and I think most of those in attendance would have agreed. Maybe this was my way of helping to keep her memory alive and having her involvement in some aspect of such a joyous day – other people may find the emotions too contradictory given similar circumstances. One thing I will be eternally grateful for is that dad was

there for the wedding – and I have the photos and DVD
of us all as a constant memory to enjoy.

Before we finally move on from the wedding, I must
just share one last thing with you. It was a piece of
writing by Alfred Pederson entitled *"The art of marriage"*. Although it is not central to the general theme
of this book I think the sentiments are worth sharing
at any time:

A good marriage must be created.
In the marriage, the little things are the big things.
It is never being too old to hold hands.
It is remembering to say "I love you"
at least once a day.
It is never going to sleep angry.
It is having a mutual sense of values
and common objectives.
It is standing together and facing the world.
It is forming a circle of love that
gathers in the whole family.
It is speaking words of appreciation
and demonstrating gratitude in thoughtful ways.
It is having the capacity to forgive and forget.
It is giving each other an atmosphere in
which each can grow.
It is a common search for the good and the beautiful.
It is not only marrying the right person, it is
being the right partner.

Linda and I had this as the reading at the wedding ceremony and as the years have passed I believe we have
followed its guidance and are fortunate to have a very
loving and happy marriage.

It is interesting to reflect on the fact that one week can encapsulate such extreme emotions – the lows of the consecration ceremony to the highs of a wedding day. Maybe the learning point is that even at the worst of times the possibility of good times may not be that far away – endure the worst times with whatever fortitude you can muster and enjoy the good times to their full.

Shortly after the wedding we flew off to the Spice Island Resort on the Caribbean island of Grenada for our honeymoon – a welcome, tranquil break after all of the recent events – returning at the end of June. Even on our honeymoon we would ring home on a regular basis to ensure everything was okay there.

The end of July brought a big, positive change. The new dialysis centre at West Byfleet had opened and dad went for his first session there on 30th July. I went along with him for the first session to ensure everything went smoothly (that he had a bed rather than a reclining chair, correct needles and length of time for the dialysis etc.). Jacqueline was taking a few, well earned, days break away in Greece at that time with Andreas. It was such a breath of fresh air to see this centre – compared with the main St Helier's Hospital. It was actually located on a small industrial park, had a pleasant reception/waiting area (with a flat screen television on the wall), with the main unit being on the ground floor. On the first floor there were offices and rooms for doctor's appointments etc. This meant that even for dad's occasional renal doctor's clinic with Dr Marsh he no longer had to go to St Helier's Hospital, but could attend here on the West Byfleet site. The main area of the dialysis unit was excellent – bright and airy, with each bed/dialysis chair having its own personal television suspended from the ceiling (with a remote for the patient) and with a socket for individual head-phones in the wall just behind the bed. Part way through each session the staff would come round and give each patient a hot drink and a choice of biscuits. It always sticks in my memory that a young lady called Iris was the nurse who put dad onto dialysis that first time. Little could I know that just over five years later she would also be the nurse who took dad off dialysis for the last time!

The atmosphere in the centre was so different from the main hospital. Because there were a limited number of patients and a small number of staff it was more like a family, with everyone knowing each other and getting on well together. Although Iris was dad's "named" nurse (each patient had a particular nurse who had overall responsibility for them) a number of other nurses regu-larly placed him on dialysis and took him off at the end, and we got to know them all well – birthday cards and cake would appear for both staff and patient birthdays, so the whole place had a family feel. A much more pleasant, relaxing and peaceful environment compared with a normal hospital ward. One of the assistants (who would carry on to qualify fully as a dialysis nurse) was Bart Nasiolkowski. He and dad struck up a close friend-ship over the years, as we all did with him and his family. Whenever dad came in for dialysis he made sure he had exactly the various pillows he needed, helped get his headset out and set up and help him take his shoes off and get comfortable on the bed ready for the session.

Transport was now a different ball game. Dad was now normally taken in by car, rather than ambulance transport, only needing to pick up another one or two people (at most). It was usually the same driver as well, so again this led to the building of a relationship rather than having a "nameless" person transporting you in. It also meant that he was picked up later on dialysis days due to the much shorter journey time, which made it more of an afternoon rather than a whole day event as previously experienced. Either Jacqueline or I would drive over to the centre and pick him up around five o'clock when he was finished and whisk him home in about twenty minutes. These changes had, I believe, an appreciable effect on dad's health and I am sure extended his remaining time with us significantly (as well as providing a better quality of life given the circumstances).

Chapter 5

The remainder of 2007 went off reasonably well (everything is relative). The big focus was on dad's 90th birthday – on 16th October. There were to be two fitting "celebrations" as such a milestone deserves. The first would take place just over a week before his actual birthday and after ninety years it would be a first – a two night break to Amsterdam and back on the inaugural cruise of the Norwegian Gem. The other would be a party at home in Bagshot inviting numerous friends and relatives both from Leeds and locally.

I seem to remember that the cruise was Jacqueline's idea. Mum and water had never gone well together, so the option of a cruise whilst mum was alive was never really a possibility. Jacqueline and I had both cruised before and had been blown away by the five star facilities of these leviathans of the sea. This particular cruise also fitted in perfectly with dad's dialysis sessions. It left Dover on Saturday afternoon and returned Monday morning. Hence, he could have his normal Friday dialysis session and then we arranged with the centre for him to be able to go in slightly later on Monday, on our return, for his afternoon session.

We left Bagshot around lunchtime on the Saturday and drove down to the Dover cruise terminal in good time. Fortunately it was a clear blue sky and showed off the gleaming new ship to its full – all 93,000 tonnes (with a capacity for approximately 2,400 guests and over 1,150 crew)! I think dad was blown away by the sheer size of it. The last time he had been on a ship (as opposed to a ferry) was when he and his parents came over from Australia when he was a child – he always used to mention that ship (the Largs Bay – a mixed passenger/cargo vessel) and the fact that it was just around 8,500 tonnes – so the Norwegian Gem was more than ten times the size! We needed to take both my car and Jacqueline's as there were five adults (including Linda and Andreas) and a lot of luggage! Not so much clothes, but all the other items such as a wheelchair, Zimmer frame etc. We managed to get everything on board and settled in. Jacqueline had arranged a disabled cabin for dad and two other cabins – one for her and Andreas and one for Linda and I, both nearby on the same deck. The whole cruise was a unique experience for dad, with the amazing facilities on board – restaurants, shows in the theatre, amazing lounges and bars etc., – and the pleasure of visiting Amsterdam again. I had taken mum and him over to Amsterdam for a day trip many years before. I think it also gave dad a boost to realise that even at ninety and with the ties and restrictions of dialysis, there were new, enjoyable experiences to be had and that he could get away from the house for short periods of time.

Because his actual birthday fell on a Tuesday. We arranged the party for the following Saturday evening. Hazel and Jim came down from Yorkshire on the Friday evening and stayed with Linda and I over the weekend. Jacqueline and I had tried to keep some of the elements of the day from dad as a surprise. There was an amazing spread of food, set up in the conservatory at Jacqueline's place and we had a speciality cake made for this unique occasion as well (along with sparklers in the shape of the numbers nine and zero), loads of balloons and I even had a couple of T shirts made with a photo of dad and I in our respective graduation gowns with "Ian's 90th Birthday" emblazoned across them!

Fortunately the response from people coming from out of town had been exceptionally good. My cousin Leslie and his wife would be there, along with a raft of friends and relatives from around Leeds. Also, local people dropped in from time to time, to make it an extra special day. The whole day was rounded off by taking dad outside, sitting him on a chair and then lighting a complete box unit of fireworks which gave an amazing display over the next few minutes. Although there were loads of presents given that day I always remember the one Hazel and Jim bought for him. It was a lovely sandy coloured blanket – very light in weight but very warm and soft. This would become a permanent item in his bag to take and use at dialysis right up until the end.

As all the changes of the past year or so had finally started to settle down, I was considering taking up work again – after all I was still only fifty two and I had also started to feel somewhat "stodgy" mentally with not having the business challenges and decision making I had been used to throughout my career. From talking to another ex-British Airways colleague, Angelo Jayawardena, I found out that he was carrying out some aviation consultancy work through an organisation called JCBA (John Bowell Associates). I made contact with the owner John Bowell and arranged to meet him at one of the hotels near Gatwick on 11th October. We seemed to hit it off and by the end of the meeting he said there was definitely work he had contracted that would benefit from my skills. I had indicated that at this stage I was only looking to work part time (given the situation with dad, Jacqueline still working full time etc.,) and he felt that would fit with his requirements as well. So, on the morning of the 12th November, virtually a year and a half after taking early retirement from British Airways and losing mum, I found myself flying out to Prague to join John's team working on some cost and strategy consulting work for Czech Airlines.

The work on Czech Airlines involved working either two or three days a week in Prague over the next six weeks, which necessitated some tweaks at home to ensure dad was still taken care of as necessary. We were fortunate that Jacqueline had a very close friend called Carol (also ex-British Airways), who lived nearby in Windlesham. She agreed to help out on the dialysis mornings I happened to be away working and came in to help dad get ready, give him his breakfast and ensure he got off to dialysis as planned. Although I continued carrying out some work in relation to Czech Airlines in January, this was virtually all done by working from home, so it did not impact greatly on my time with dad.

The winter period was always a concern regarding dialysis. Although we now had a significantly reduced journey time we were still at the vagaries of the weather. There was little leeway in terms of being able to delay dialysis, plus the fact that the centre itself had sessions booked with different patients each morning and afternoon – so there was not a lot of slack in the system to accommodate moving people from one day/session to another. Snow was the real killer. Fortunately in Surrey the episodes of heavy snowfall were few and far between (it would have been a very different story in Yorkshire). Jacqueline lived on a large estate with a long inclined road coming up from the main road. Laird Court was just off this main road (as a cul-de-sac). There were a number of occasions when we had to get the snow shovels out to clear the area near her house so a car (and dad) could get in and out. Generally we would be able to use a car, but there was one episode I remember when the snowfall was particularly heavy. Fortunately, the dialysis centre managed to gain access to some large 4x4 patient transport vehicles which were better at accessing such roads in that weather. It was a struggle, but they still managed to get dad to and from dialysis that day. Unless you are involved with someone requiring time critical medical support it is hard to impart the level of anxiety that a simple thing such as a snowfall can instil.

Although the dialysis had been going reasonably, an issue did surface in early 2008. Every few months each patient would be checked to ensure the blood flow was strong enough and in early 2008 they detected that dad's flow was slower than required. From further tests they had identified that there was a small "kink" further up the arm in one of the veins linked to the fistula. This was slowing down the blood flow which causes issues in trying to dialyse successfully. They decided to undertake a venoplasty procedure – this entails putting a wire into the vein and using a balloon type mechanism to try and carefully straighten out the kink/open up the vein. This was an extremely delicate procedure as if they damaged the vein in any way then the fistula would be rendered useless with all the immediate and extreme implications thereof.

The actual procedure was undertaken under a local anaesthetic at St Helier's Hospital on 6th March. Jacqueline and I were both there with dad to give moral and physical support. The time taken to carry out the procedure was not long (I seem to remember about forty five minutes) and fortunately when the doctors came out to say we could come back in to help dad get ready to go, they indicated they believed the procedure had been a complete success – however, the final proof would be follow up measurements of the flow in the coming weeks. The only concern as we left the hospital is that they indicated that such "kinks" could recur, so the straightening out may only last for about a year. In fact, as with many time estimates we had concerning dad, it lasted through the rest of his years on dialysis with no further problems arising.

Early in February Linda and I had managed a week's break over in Florida, staying with some friends who live just outside Orlando, and around Easter time in March Jacqueline spent some time over in Greece with Andreas. Whenever, Jacqueline went away I would move into Laird Court to look after dad. Usually Linda also stayed with me at the weekends, but during the week she would remain at home and come over after finishing work in the evenings.

It is worth pausing to reflect on the impact these periods of live-in caring had on me emotionally. When you have someone you are responsible for looking after there is always an increased level of stress associated with that – whether it is a baby, older person or someone in between. Such a transition did not come naturally to me, albeit while there was somebody else there in the house the stress levels were lower. Personally this was for two reasons. The practical one was that my cooking skills are very basic and so having Linda there to cook the main meals was a great weight off my shoulders! If Jacqueline was away I wanted to ensure that dad felt well looked after and that he had meals he would enjoy as part of that (albeit he only had a small appetite). The other, more impactful aspect, was if a medical problem should occur. If there is nobody else there and a medical issue arises it can be significantly more difficult to deal with. For example, if an angina attack occurred then one person could be administering dad's spray and staying with him, whilst the other one could be getting the oxygen we had in the house.

Also, in coming to a difficult decision, such as having to call an ambulance, the ability to talk the situation through with someone else was a great benefit. Despite the fact that Jacqueline and I constantly impressed on dad that, should he feel he had a problem or needed some help at any time, he must call for us, there were occasions (particularly during the night) where he did not do that. Consequently, I was particularly aware of the heightened level of stress during the night, if Linda wasn't there. Sometimes I would be in bed and think I heard the sound the GTN spray would make if used. I would quietly get out of bed and go to dad's bedroom to see if he was awake/had used the spray. Most times, fortunately, that was not the case, but sometimes he would be having some chest pain and was using the spray!! Hence, I was always a light sleeper when I was standing in for Jacqueline in this respect.

I think also, being in a house that isn't your own can be quite unsettling – you aren't familiar where everything is, nor do you have all your belongings to hand, which is far more restrictive than looking after someone in your own home. Although we haven't talked about these reflections specifically, I am sure that Jacqueline would have felt the same when she was on her own in the house with dad. With her husband travelling to Greece on a regular basis (usually spending up to a week at a time there on business, or longer for family/leisure purposes) there were plenty of times when she was the only person at home looking after dad (albeit most times I would only be a few minutes away down the road in case of a problem).

As I am "reflecting" at this point it is also worth pausing on the topic of physical interaction when you lose someone close. After mum's passing Jacqueline and I still had our other halves for physical intimacy, support and comfort – yet dad had lost that one person he had shared that intimacy with most of his life. He could no longer hold mum's hand in bed at night or have someone give him a hug etc. Often in these situations family, friends and carers can miss this aspect of loss and care, focussing more on the practical day to day matters such as washing, making meals, general company etc. For any tactile person though, the loss of this aspect of their lives could have a very negative and depressing effect over time. Although you can never replace that level of intimacy, a number of us around dad tried to maintain as much of that contact as possible – obviously Jacqueline the most; I always gave dad a kiss on the cheek whenever I came in and Linda always did the same. Friends and family from Leeds, like Moira and my cousin Leslie also were tactile in that way which I believed helped. As I have said above – it is a very easy aspect of loss that can be missed going forward.

Returning to the day to day story, we finally had a success with the completion of the flat sale in Leeds. Again, this had nearly fallen through at the last minute (for the fourth time), but due mainly to some exceptional help from the estate agents Manning Stainton we saw this one through to the bitter end. Finally on 11th April 2008 the flat was sold and the money transferred to dad's bank account – it had taken well over a year and a half to make it happen. Again, in hindsight we were fortunate to conclude the sale when we did as with the economic crisis imminent the value of the property would have only continued to decline over the following few years! There were mixed feelings though, especially for dad, as although we were pleased everything had finally been concluded and tied up it was tinged with the sadness of knowing his last home with mum had finally gone.

I carried out some further Czech Airlines work during April, but this was interrupted by a major health problem with dad. It started one Friday evening at the end of April. I had picked him up from dialysis and was coming back home through Windlesham when he said he was starting to feel sick. I thought initially it was probably just the effects at the end of a week's dialysis – but not so. By the time we got back to Laird Court he was actually being sick. I had called ahead to let Jacqueline know and she was there waiting on the door step with a sick bowl to help. We managed to get dad inside and settled into his armchair. After a while as things seemed to be calming down I left for home, but it wasn't long before I got a call from Jacqueline saying the situation was getting worse and dad was complaining of pain in the lower part of the abdomen. I went straight back and shortly afterwards we had to call an ambulance and found ourselves on the way to Frimley Park Hospital (our local hospital about ten to fifteen minutes away). Jacqueline went in the ambulance with dad and I followed on behind having grabbed a number of items we may need at the hospital – including medication, pyjamas and slippers, his light blanket etc., etc. Unfortunately, this was a split of responsibilities Jacqueline and I would re-enact a few times over the coming years.

Again, one piece of advice I would give to anyone in a similar position is to type up details of the person's medication, including dosage and when they start/stop any medication, details of any items they are allergic to (e.g. penicillin) and key personal details such as full name, date of birth etc. Jacqueline and I each kept a copy of this and we tended to have a spare copy that we could immediately give to a doctor at any hospital, which helped expedite proceedings and minimised the risk of omissions/errors. The other key reason one of us needed to be with dad was the fact that most medical personnel will use the left arm of a person to take blood pressure readings (as most people are right handed). This was an absolute "no no" as regards dad, as that was the arm he had his fistula in. The likelihood was that taking blood pressure from that arm would "blow" the fistula and cause major problems. On more than one occasion we saved dad from such an outcome by the skin of our teeth, despite always ensuring this was written down on his notes etc., when in hospital!

The diagnosis for dad was not good. He had inflammation in his abdominal region, to an extent that under normal circumstances he would have had surgery to remove the underlying problem. However, given his heart, kidney and general conditions (along with low blood pressure) the doctors believed there was a high risk of him not surviving the operation. They decided instead to pump him full of high dosage antibiotics (intravenously) and hope that over time they would combat the source of the infection/inflammation – if not ......! He would end up spending the next two and a half weeks in hospital fighting to recover, which threw up significant additional problems in terms of him receiving dialysis on a regular basis. At that time Frimley Park did not have full dialysis facilities. Had they had such a capability all that would have been required would have been for dad's bed to be wheeled from his normal ward to the dialysis ward as required and then back again once his dialysis had been completed. Instead, the logistics to get him dialysed either at the West Byfleet satellite or back at the main St Helier's Hospital were to prove monumental (and detrimental to his fight to recover).

As he was admitted on a Friday night it was not until Monday that we faced the first issue regarding dialysis. We had been in discussion with the nursing staff regarding arranging transport to and from the West Byfleet centre, who had agreed to continue carrying out his sessions subject to any further issues arising. Transport was needed as dad would need to go on a stretcher and have oxygen to hand as well – so a normal seated transport vehicle would not suffice. The transport was booked to collect him from the ward in order to arrive at West Byfleet between 12:00 and 12:30 p.m. The journey would normally take about half an hour. Despite all the arrangements and confirmations for the Monday, come the day he was not picked up from Ward F8 until about 2:30 p.m. (already two hours late for his treatment session) – and did not arrive at West Byfleet until approximately 3 p.m. It was confirmed that return transport had been booked and that he would be ready by 7 p.m. for the return.

The dialysis went without incident and being ready at the agreed time we continued to await transport. During the evening the staff at the dialysis centre rang both Frimley Park and GSL (the transport organisation) on several occasions to chase the return transport. The F8 Ward staff also chased transport for a return time confirmation. Throughout this no return time would be communicated by GSL – just that he would be picked up sometime!! Despite the dialysis unit making clear the fact that they would be closing the facility at around 11 p.m. (as they are an independent non-hospital unit – with no doctor on site) GSL continued to evade any indication of a pickup time. Come eleven o'clock two of the dialysis staff agreed to remain with Ian until the situation was resolved (definitely going above and beyond the call of duty). At that stage contact was made with the Frimley Park Site Manager. Despite her best efforts talking to GSL she indicated that both the two crew ambulances were on their way to London and could still be some considerable time away from any pick up.

After detailed discussions (despite being a further risk to Ian's health) it was agreed that the Site Manager (Mary) would order a "disabled" taxi (using her own credit card to do so I believe) which could have a wheelchair "wheeled" straight into it and that dad would be accompanied by Jacqueline on the journey. As he was on oxygen the dialysis staff generously agreed to loan/provide an oxygen cylinder (and the wheelchair) to facilitate this – we committed to returning both early the following morning (ready for their morning dialysis shift).

The taxi finally arrived around midnight and dad eventually reached Frimley Park around half past midnight. Due to lack of prompt return he had missed key medication for his condition and so had to be administered this (some via a drip) on return to the ward – despite being in the early hours of the morning. Jacqueline and I finally got to bed around 2:30 a.m. and then had to be up early the next day to return the oxygen/equipment to West Byfleet by about eight o'clock that morning! The whole episode throughout the evening/journey back to Frimley Park inflicted major stress/upset and physical detriment to dad (who was reduced to tears at one point late in the evening – something virtually unheard of for him).

By the time we got to the following Saturday (3rd May) dad's condition had deteriorated to a level that the doctor's decided it would not be safe for him to continue dialysing at West Byfleet and that this should take place at the main St Helier's Hospital (at Carshalton) – as there was full medical support there if required.

Again Ward F8 at Frimley Park correctly made the transport booking with GSL for out/return journeys, stipulating stretcher/oxygen requirements and a family member to accompany in the ambulance.

As this would be a much longer journey and the fact that St Helier's were squeezing dad in to an already busy dialysis schedule, pick up had been arranged at 7:30 a.m. to be at St Helier's by 9 a.m. – he was not picked up from Ward F8 until approximately 9:30 a.m. and did not reach St Helier's until 10:30 a.m. (already an hour and a half late for his treatment session). Again, it was confirmed that return transport had been booked and towards the end of the dialysis session the staff on the ward confirmed with GSL that Ian would be ready by 6 p.m. – however, when chased later they indicated it would probably by around 7:30 p.m. for the pickup. The transport actually arrived at 8 p.m. They saw Ian was on oxygen and said they had not been advised of that requirement and did not have enough on-board for the journey back to Frimley Park! They also said they had not been advised of the family member accompanying Ian in the ambulance.

Despite the ward sister ringing all around the hospital to try and find an oxygen cylinder that was compatible with the ambulance no such equipment could be found (it appears the fittings on the ambulance are different from any oxygen cylinders used at St Helier's Hospital)!! Consequently, the ambulance crew said they had no option but to go to their base in Dorking, pick up a full oxygen cylinder and then return – they indicated this would be at least an hour or so. They left at 8:30 p.m. and did not return until 10:20 p.m. Finally they got dad on board and we arrived at Frimley Park just before 11:30 p.m. On reaching the ward Ian was complaining of kidney/back pain and had to be administered pain killing medication as well as his usual medication (which, again, he had missed). I should stress throughout the above that the medical/nursing staff at Frimley Park Hospital did everything in their powers to look after and help Ian – the above is in no way a reflection on their excellent care. In contrast the organisation and operation of the GSL transport service was appalling, totally unacceptable in terms of patient health/care and undoubtedly contributed to a deterioration in Ian's health (and mental state/anxiety).

Sometimes unfortunate events can happen as a one off, but this second episode indicated to Jacqueline and I that we could place no trust in the transport system as supplied/arranged via the hospital and we decided to take matters into our own hands. I think it might have been while I was recounting the events during a telephone call with my cousin Leslie in Leeds that he suggested we should consider paying for private ambulance transport. Having looked into it we rapidly went down that route (engaging a firm called AST). After dad's stay in hospital we also submitted a formal complaint to the hospital and eventually they compensated us for some of the AST costs we had to expend.

The difference was striking with AST. They were always there on time for taking Ian in and picking him up and were extremely supportive and responsive all round. I suppose that is what you pay for when you are laying out approximately £500 per round trip! In the end we had to engage them for four return trips to St Helier's and one to West Byfleet. We were fortunate that there were savings to use to provide the level of care that was required – many people would have been much less fortunate and other patients would have had to bear the detrimental effects of such an incompetent transport organisation. Such shortcomings are simply unacceptable – after all it is not rocket science to organise the required transport and associated facilities at an agreed time!

After these incidents the hospital did discuss another option with us – that of them transferring him to St Helier's Hospital. The benefit would obviously be that all the care would be under one roof and would obviate the need for transport between the two locations. Jacqueline and I discussed this long and hard. The upside was obvious, but there were significant downsides – not least was the fact that Frimley Park had an excellent reputation as a Foundation Trust, pleasant wards, easy access for us to provide continual support etc. At that time Epsom & St Helier's Hospital had not achieved the required standards to become a Foundation Trust and had a very poor reputation. We did discuss the pros and cons with dad, but with having found the AST option for transport we decided to go with the best medical care reputation and ease of access/support – so dad remained at Frimley Park.

Dad's stay in hospital was traumatic for medical as well as transport reasons. The medical staff used two different high dosage antibiotic treatments over a couple of weeks to try and clear the inflammation. Some of the effects on dad were to "knock him out" and also cause delusions and hallucinations etc. At one stage he was refusing to eat the food as he kept saying it had been poisoned! From other fragmented communications it became clear he thought he was back fighting in World War II and that the food had been tampered with. The staff on the ward were extremely accommodating and allowed us great flexibility in coming in to help dad. Jacqueline would regularly come in at breakfast time and bring food for him etc. Having seemed to be going downhill at one stage he eventually turned the corner and slowly started to recover. At the lowest point our cousin Leslie made a special journey down from Leeds to visit Ian – as we genuinely did not know whether he would be afforded another opportunity to see him. However, at last, after around two and a half weeks, we heaved a sigh of relief as on 13th May the hospital agreed to discharge Ian. The only sting in the tail was that they indicated such an infection/inflammation could recur at any time – so in a way we all potentially had a time bomb in our midst. On the upside West Byfleet had agreed dad could resume dialysis there – a big fillip for all of us.

On the part time work front I had indicated to JCBA (when dad was taken into hospital) that I would not be available for a while. The way things worked out I only did about four more (part time) weeks of work on Czech Airlines around July that year. Although the consulting work was interesting and enjoyable, I decided that it would be more effective to pursue a full time role for a couple of years or so instead. I had been looking out for the right opportunity to take my eye and then suddenly in May I saw an advert from Monitor (the health sector regulator) looking for Senior Relationship Managers. Monitor had responsibility at that time for assessing NHS Trusts and awarding then Foundation Trust (FT) status should they meet the required standards. Once authorised an FT would be assigned a Relationship Manager and Senior Relationship Manager. They would be responsible for ongoing contact between Monitor, as the regulator, and the FT and would risk assess the FT on an ongoing basis – proposing regulatory action to be taken should issues arise. This seemed an ideal fit considering my skill set. The last role I held at British Airways had been Head of Risk Control and Programme Management, plus my detailed financial background and experience of working at senior/ Board level was a good fit for the position.

To cut a long story short (and a couple of interviews later) I was offered a Senior Relationship Manager position. However, I would not be required to take this up until November 2008 – that would be nearly two years after we moved dad down to Surrey and two and a half years since I left British Airways – they say time flies! This wait also gave Jacqueline and I the opportunity to decide how we would adjust matters to continue to provide dad with the care he required. As things turned out the period when Jacqueline and I were both working full time would only last for about six or seven months, as subsequently she took the opportunity to take early retirement from British Airways at the end of May 2009 (after twenty four years). Her bosses at British Airways were extremely supportive as well, and they agreed to her working one day a week from home plus she started later on some other days. This, along with her friend Carol's help, saw us through the "overlap" period until she retired.

Having had this severe scare in April/May it took a little while for dad to really recover and get his strength back. Although Ian would "bounce back" a number of times from medical problems, it started to become evident that each time the recovery did not take him back to how he was beforehand, but always seemed to plateau at a slightly lower level – I suppose objectively that should not have been a surprise as poor health and traumas take their toll on the body at any age, let alone when someone is in their nineties. The deterioration manifested itself in the likes of mobility – both the distance he could move around and the support required. For example, getting up the two steps on Jacqueline's front path to her house became even more of a challenge.

In that respect we finally hit on a beneficial solution. Jacqueline had been considering ways of alleviating the problem, but various issues seemed to arise. Due to the nature of her front path it was not as simple to address the issue as it had been for Linda and I at our house (by making the path a long, gentle slope rather than having intermittent steps in it). It was becoming quite urgent to address this issue when suddenly my regular journey to work threw up a potential solution. I commuted in to London from Woking on South West Trains and one day had noticed that the guards at the station were helping someone in a wheelchair at the station onto a train using a metal portable ramp. "Eureka" as they say! Next time I was at Jacqueline's I measured up the various horizontal and vertical distances between the steps on the path. Although it seemed unlikely that a single ramp would be practical, the use of two smaller ramps could well work. I had mentioned this to Linda, who worked for an industrial flooring company over at Godalming. She indicated that they did sell such ramps, of various sizes, and she discussed the matter with the technical staff at her work to see whether my proposal would work/should be safe given the strength/limits of the ramps. The answer was yes and the added benefit was that the company had a smaller ramp as a display item and offered to give that to Linda for free, plus she would be able to get a seventy five percent discount on the longer ramp – a significant saving as the longer versions of these ramps can cost in excess of £500! As dad was adamant that he would pay for anything we acquired we discussed it with him and got his agreement to go ahead – it was a great success and a real god send, especially when we sometimes had to use the wheelchair to get him in and out of the house when he was not too well.

Again, this was another example of where having some savings and paying for items yourself can solve a problem quickly. It would probably have been possible to obtain a similar solution through local government (social services), but would no doubt have taken many months of bureaucracy and frustration – that is not equitable, but does seem to be a reflection of reality currently.

On a more positive note Jacqueline had been looking into the possibility of a further break/holiday for dad – longer than just a weekend as per the cruise the previous year. That would necessitate him dialysing somewhere near the destination we chose. There was an administrative facility attached to the hospital that helped provide advice and arrange such temporary sessions. There was a small facility just near Bournemouth, located in a house that had the capability to dialyse three or four people at a time. Jacqueline managed to arrange a week's worth of sessions down there for the week commencing 30th June. Obviously, there was some trepidation as this would be the first time dad had dialysed away from a main hospital or centre. Fortunately our fears proved to be unfounded and the dialysis went off without a hitch that week.

Dad, Jacqueline, Linda and I went down to Bournemouth on Saturday 28th June. Again we took two cars due to the large amount of items we needed for dad. I think Andreas had decided to go off to Greece during that week. We stayed at a reasonable hotel on the clifftop road just outside Bournemouth, with a great view out to sea and back to the centre of the town. Jacqueline shared a twin room with dad and Linda and I had a double nearby. Linda had taken the Monday and Tuesday off as leave from work, so we had four days down there before we returned home on Tuesday evening (I was flying off to Prague on business on the Wednesday for a couple of days). I then returned on the Saturday to help Jacqueline bring everything back. It proved to be a very enjoyable time, helped by the weather being generally good. Dad had a reasonable level of independence as well, as we brought down his mobility scooter (we had bought him this as a present the previous year). It meant that he could enjoy going along the promenade or the pier without having to rely on one of us pushing him in the wheelchair. Meals out and visits to places around and outside Bournemouth made for a good break away. After everything that had taken place in April/May that year this must have been a real boost to dad a couple of months later to have a proper holiday away from home.

Having mentioned the mobility scooter we bought for dad, it is worth noting that a lot of towns have "Shopmobility" type schemes which can be helpful for anyone with mobility problems. We had used the one in Woking a number of times. Generally the person pays a small amount for membership and then a reduced amount each type they wish to use a scooter. In Woking they had a location at the top of the main Peacocks Shopping Centre. It proved ideal in allowing dad some feeling of independence in getting around the shops, it meant Jacqueline or I did not have to push him in a wheelchair and also it gave us all the opportunity to try out such a facility before deciding to buy one of our own (a version which could be taken apart quickly to carry in a car boot and then quickly re-assembled wherever we went).

Over the summer Jacqueline managed a couple of short breaks away herself. She and Andreas spent a few days in Greece during the last week in July and then visited Stockholm for a wedding at the end of the first week in August. During their first break Moira Gelman came down from Leeds and visited dad, with us all going out for a meal locally in the evening. Linda and I had our main holiday during the first couple of weeks of September – visiting the Bahamas, staying at a hotel just outside Nassau on the beach. Unfortunately, that did not prove to be the restful holiday we anticipated. As you may know the period from around June/July to October is the peak season for hurricanes in the Caribbean. Although everything was fine during the first few days of the holiday we were then advised that there was a hurricane warning and that one of the storms tracking across the Atlantic could catch the Bahamas on its way through. As the days went by the likelihood of a hit became greater, to the extent that the hotel was making arrangements to board up windows (not a good sign) and also advised guests that should they wish to leave earlier than planned they would "credit" their remaining days so they could be used at some future date.

As the boarding of windows started to take place we decided to be conservative and take a flight across to Florida for the remaining days of our holiday (we could then return home from Miami). As good as their word, the hotel provided us with documentation entitling us to return and use up our remaining days at any time over the following year. We would end up returning the following March, albeit that visit ended up with an even more traumatic event (which I will explain later).

The autumn of 2008 was relatively uneventful. There was one visit to Leeds for all of us, involving visiting mum's grave and again meeting up with friends and family. We had settled into staying at the same hotel now – the Holiday Inn at Garforth, which was just off the M1 motorway on the way in to Leeds and was convenient to get to the north side of Leeds where most of the friends and relatives lived. It was often during such visits that spectres of the past arose. There was a very good fish and chip restaurant on Street Lane in Leeds called Marlow's, which we frequented many times over the years. Sitting there on one of our visits did bring back some sadness, as I pictured us sat at the same table with mum and dad in years gone by – now there was one person less at the table. I suppose it is inevitable that such emotions will surface from time to time as you re-visit favourite locations, but it doesn't make coming to terms with the situation any easier.

Back in Surrey things had been moving on. Dad was an avid reader and had collected a wide array of books over the years. He had decided that it would be nice to have a proper array of fitted bookshelves in his bedroom at Laird Court. Fortunately, the husband (Mel) of one of Jacqueline's friends from British Airways was a carpenter and sat down with dad to agree a design for what he wanted. He made an excellent job and this certainly added a more personal touch to dad's room. We had also identified a Masonic Lodge fairly close by in Aldershot and dad started to attend that once a month on a fairly regular basis. Initially Jacqueline would take him over and often I would pick him up. Despite working full time, I did on occasions take a half day's leave (as meetings were early evening on a Tuesday) and actually go along with him. He had always enjoyed the craft and the social interaction as always gave him a lift.

On the medical front we had also managed to obtain a standalone oxygen machine (we already had a small portable oxygen cylinder which would go on the back of the wheelchair) which proved invaluable in the years to come. If dad had an angina attack or just started to feel short of breath we could switch this on for him to use and there was no cylinder to exchange/refill. However, obtaining the machine proved somewhat of a merry-go-round initially, as everyone we talked to indicated that it was someone else that needed to give the approval (another story, not for this book)!! Unfortunately, the need for this facility was becoming more necessary as during 2008 the number of angina episodes we recorded rose to ten, from about half that in the previous year (and was to double again in 2009). We also all made sure that we had flu jabs as we wanted to minimise the possibility of dad catching something from one of us (he had enough challenges medically)!

However, just before I started work at Monitor on 10th November we had another lurch in the roller coaster ride when dad had a more severe angina attack.

It happened on the afternoon of Tuesday 4th November. The GTN spray and oxygen didn't do the trick on this occasion and I had to call for an ambulance. It always gave you that sinking feeling when you had to call for an ambulance – knowing that would start a long sequence of events/time at hospital, possible dialysis and transport problems etc. On this occasion they just kept him in a couple of nights and tested to see whether he had experienced a heart attack rather than a severe angina attack. Fortunately, the tests came back negative and they let Ian home on Thursday 6th November.

As the year came towards a close it was time for my birthday and Andreas's (our birthdays being a day apart on 29th and 30th November respectively). As it was Andreas's 60th birthday Jacqueline arranged for them to fly out to San Francisco (somewhere he had expressed an interest in visiting) for a long weekend break. They left on 28th November and arrived back on the Tuesday afternoon of 2nd December. However, after a good break away they arrived back to the GP leaving Laird Court! As a celebration of my birthday dad, Linda and I had gone out on the Saturday evening to a top quality restaurant in Chobham (just ten minutes away). It appeared the liver that dad had as a main course did not agree with him – whether it was not cooked properly still remains a mystery to this day. Over the next forty eight hours this disagreement surfaced quite violently and necessitated getting the GP out to see him. Not exactly the enjoyable celebration we had hoped for!

Chapter 6

2009 started off without particular incident albeit, as mentioned above, dad's angina episodes started to become more frequent than in the past. Despite the fact that it was winter, there were still opportunities to take him out from time to time with visits to the cinema and theatre. In the first quarter of 2009 there were a couple of trips to the Royal Festival Hall in London. Going up to London always brought back happy memories for Ian as he had undertaken his degree at Royal College there many years ago. On occasions, as well, there was the odd film that would be of interest – such as a new Star Trek movie – to which we could all go.

Linda was starting to get more concerned about her mother's health as well. Although her mum (Joyce) was only in her seventies she seemed to be having a continuing problem since late 2008 which was giving her pain, causing her to lose some weight etc. She did go into hospital in March and although they detected some signs of cancer the prognosis initially wasn't too bad. We were due to have a week back in the Bahamas from 6th March (using up the "credited" days left from our visit the previous September). We did consider whether to postpone the trip, but things seemed to be reasonably stable down in Taunton (where Linda's parents lived) and after talking to them she decided to go ahead with the break. The holiday went well, with good weather (the hurricane season had long gone), until the day we were due to come back. That Friday 13th certainly lived up to its superstitious reputation.

The day started out as normal and we wandered downstairs for a good breakfast at Sandals Royal Bahamian Resort. We got back to the room and began to get ready for the last morning around the pool when the phone rang. I picked it up and it was Linda's brother Eddie at the other end. My heart sank, as he would only call us in an emergency situation and as we were due back in the UK the following morning it was obvious it must be something extremely serious. He told me the news and asked to speak to Linda – she took over the phone and there was silence for a few moments and then she dissolved onto the bed into distraught tears. Her mum had suddenly deteriorated rapidly and passed away in hospital! I picked up the phone and had a further sombre conversation with Eddie. The next flight back to London was the one we were booked on late that evening, which would get back around lunch-time on the Saturday. I expressed my heartfelt condolences to him and said we would call him as soon as we were back home tomorrow to discuss what the arrangements would be going forward. Unlike with my mother, there was not the time pressure of needing to go ahead with the funeral within the next forty eight hours so when we got back the family could discuss what arrangements they wished to make.

I came off the phone and just held Linda who was sobbing her heart out. I knew exactly how she felt – it was less than three years since I had experienced the same trauma. It is bad enough anyway when such events take place, but when it comes as a surprise rather than after a period of expectation it is even more of a shock to the system. I knew that there was absolutely nothing I could say to take away any of the pain. In those situations the best thing is simply to be there for the other person and to provide any physical or emotional comfort they need. We needed to check out of the room by lunchtime and solemnly packed everything up. I had a word with the hotel management to explain the situation that had arisen and asked if there was some kind of courtesy room we could use during the day rather than having to sit out around the pool the whole time. They were very helpful and understanding and found us some accommodation where we could have more privacy. Also, they said they would arrange one of their private cars to take us to the airport that evening.

In hindsight that enforced time before we could go home may have been beneficial. It gave us some time to calmly talk about things and the sort of arrangements and timings that would probably ensue over the next week or two. Hopefully, it gave Linda that space to start to get her mind around what had happened before being thrown into the midst of everything on our return. Again, my mind turned back to that day in Leeds in 2006 when I lost my mum. The weather was lovely then, but yet the world felt horribly cold due to that loss. I knew that despite being under the beautiful Caribbean skies and warmth that Linda must be feeling the same coldness.

We arrived home the next day and ended up travelling down to Taunton the following Wednesday evening.

The funeral (cremation) was held at 10:30 a.m. the following morning (19th March). There was just the immediate family there and I was pleasantly amazed at how well Linda appeared to cope with the actual service (better than I had done in Leeds). Her dad was eighty two at the time and from that time on Linda and her brother agreed that every couple of weeks they would alternate with one of them going down to Taunton for the weekend to help support him in whatever way was necessary. So that meant each of them would visit once a month – it was déjà vu of what Jacqueline and I had done over the latter years for mum and dad in Leeds.

Dad had a further brief admission to hospital in April that year, with an overnight stay from 7th to 8th April after a severe angina episode. Again, the tests showed that it was severe angina rather than a heart attack, but they decided to refer him back to a cardiologist to review the ongoing situation.

June was a busy month. There was the "*Yahrzeit*" anniversary of mum's passing (always commemorated at the synagogue) as well as a further visit to the cardiologist, June brought a welcome visit from one of our relatives in Australia – Marcia Haskin. Marcia lived in Melbourne and her late husband David (who had died of cancer some years earlier) was one of dad's cousins. We had visited them all on our three trips back to Australia in the early/mid-eighties and had seen them on their visits to the UK on occasions since then. Marcia had always stayed in touch and she and dad talked on the phone from time to time to catch up. Her term of endearment for dad was "big shit" and I was therefore "little shit" – as they say, you had to have met Marcia and been there to understand that! She arrived into Dover from a cruise on 19th June and stayed in London for a few days until she left from Heathrow on the 23rd in the evening. It was always a boost (for all of us) to meet up with our antipodean relatives and a double plus that weekend as it was also Father's Day. We also had the pleasure of some of our other relatives visiting us over the years, including Pam and Norma Harris. In fact, we saw Norma on one of her visits to the UK later in 2009. These visits were always a great fillip for dad, as it brought back memories of his childhood in Australia and our visits back there in later life. Linda and I intend to go back down under to visit the relatives and spend more time exploring Australia when we are both retired (all being well).

Linda and I got away for our main holiday in September, this time to Arizona where we had an enjoyable time staying out in the Scottsdale area and exploring quite a bit of Arizona (including Tombstone – the site of the shoot-out at the OK Corral). This time there were no calls and no emergencies thank goodness. One thing that I had learned from past experience though was to work out exactly how we would get home quickly, if necessary, from any holiday location. Phoenix wasn't a problem as there was a daily direct flight back to London. However, when we went on a cruise we would be in different ports each day (some without direct connections back to London), so I always did an appreciable amount of homework up front before we went as to exactly how we could get home should the need arise (it gave me some peace of mind).

A further short admission into hospital took place with dad in mid-October. Unfortunately, it was the day of his birthday – 17th (they say timing is everything). We had arranged for people to drop in later that day to Laird Court and there was to be the usual buffet for all to partake in – but dad's body had other ideas! There was another bout of angina in the afternoon that we could not alleviate and so had to call the ambulance. I think dad was more concerned about the disruption to everyone's plans rather than his condition, but we assured him it was no problem and that, all being well, we would re-arrange things for the following week. As back in April the hospital only kept him in overnight to rule out a more serious heart attack. As good as our word, we re-arranged the birthday celebrations for the following weekend – ninety two and counting.

He was also having to have more attention and treatment to his back and hip. Various bouts and levels of pain had been taking place over quite some time and the specialist had administered injections into the hip on more than one occasion to try and alleviate the discomfort. The bottom part of his back was identified as "deteriorating" but we were all keeping our fingers crossed that the level of deterioration would remain manageable for the length of time we needed it to.

We all made a weekend visit back to Leeds at the end of October (except Andreas who went out to Greece on the Sunday) – another chance to meet up again with various friends and relatives before the depths of winter descended upon us. And so 2009 came to a close. Christmas now took its familiar pattern, with Linda spending a few days in Taunton with her dad and brother and me being invited to spend Christmas and Boxing Day around at Jacqueline's with dad and Andreas. It wasn't until after dad passed away that

Linda and I would ever spend Christmas together. I always went to Leeds in the past to be with mum and dad (and now Jacqueline's) and Linda did the same to be with her parents down in Taunton – it would be twenty years after our meeting each other before we spent our first Christmas together!

One other situation that marked the generosity of dad (and his continual thoughts of how best to help other people) also came right at the end of 2009. It concerned the mortgage Jacqueline and Andreas still had remaining on Laird Court. I was not privy to the exact details but from what dad said their current agreement was, I believe, going to finish around the end of 2009 and they were obviously looking to take out a further one with their mortgage lender. Apparently the various policies they had, which would pay off the mortgage, matured at various times over the following few years, including when they would be over sixty five years old. Obviously, this could have had an impact on when Andreas might be able to retire. Also, they would be continuing to pay interest on the mortgage until all the policies had matured. Dad had been ruminating on this for some time (and had mentioned it to me on more than one occasion). He finally decided that, out of his savings, he would give Jacqueline the amount of money outstanding at this time (a substantial amount, as you would expect given it was a mortgage) in order that she could clear the remaining amount, save all those future interest payments and give her and Andreas more freedom to decide when he wished to retire.

In general, I was supportive of anything that helped Jacqueline, but just advised dad that we needed to ensure he still had a reasonable amount of savings left for anything that he might need going forward. He finally decided to go ahead with this action and the appropriate money was transferred to Jacqueline towards the end of December. However, that was not the end of the story.

Mum and dad had always been incredibly even handed between Jacqueline and I over the years – there was never any "favourite" between us. Whether it be money spent on weddings or the amount they gave me towards the deposit on my first flat, they would always make sure an equivalent amount went to the other sibling. Now was no different and dad insisted that he give me a cheque for the same amount as he was giving Jacqueline for the mortgage. I indicated that, fortunately, I was now in a comfortable financial position and that I would prefer he kept the money in his savings to use as required – but he absolutely insisted that I receive the same amount as Jacqueline. The "quid pro quo" I agreed was that I said I wouldn't be spending it whilst he was around and that I would put it into one of my savings accounts (so it was there for him to use in case of any extreme emergency).

The above situation was so typical of dad (and mum in the past). Despite everything he was going through and enduring he was still thinking about the best way to help other people rather than just being introverted and concentrating on himself – a very special person indeed.

As a qualified accountant my conscience can't let me move on from the above without setting out one warning comment. Under current tax law any "gifts" made within a certain number of years before someone's death still count towards the value of their estate that needs to be included on the Inheritance Tax Form (completed as part of probate, when they pass away). So generally I would suggest to people to take appropriate advice if they are contemplating similar (more complex) situations.

2010 was certainly a year for milestone birthdays. The first one was Linda's 50th in February, followed by Jacqueline's 60th in May. For Linda's we managed to arrange a family dinner out at a favourite place called Foxhills, near Ottershaw, in Surrey. It consisted of a manor house set in vast grounds that had been converted into a couple of golf courses. In the manor house there was an excellent restaurant. There was also a large lounge area with an open fire where you could relax pre and post the meal. We would have pre-dinner drinks and look at the menu beforehand and then retire to there after the meal to sit around the fire and have coffee and petit-fours – very civilised. We managed to arrange one of the Saturday evenings in early February when neither Eddie nor Linda were down at their dad's in Taunton – so there was seven of us (dad, Linda and I, Jacqueline and Andreas and Eddie and his fiancé Sue). We had a large round table in the dining room set in a big bay window. I had ordered a special birthday cake for Linda and delivered it to the restaurant earlier in the day – so coffee and petit-fours expanded into a birthday cake with sparklers etc. It was an enjoyable evening for all and I remember thinking at the time that we really had to savour every minute of such occasions as, given dad's age, we wouldn't have many opportunities left for all of us to be together in this way. For Linda's actual birthday I took her away for a spa weekend in Brockenhurst in the New Forest (the Careys Manor Hotel).

Early in March I "dad sat" for a long weekend whilst Jacqueline had a break – Linda and I had managed a week away back in February. Shortly afterwards in March we had another hospital visit with dad. Nothing to do with his angina or renal problems this time. Many years ago as a youth he had taken part in a myriad of sports including boxing. He had suffered some damage around the eyebrow area on one eye due to cuts etc. In later years it started to itch/provide some discomfort so we had arranged an appointment with a dermatologist to check it out. Long story short was that eventually they diagnosed that there was the presence of cancer in the area! Fortunately it still seemed to be localised and hadn't spread any further – Ian just didn't seem to be able to catch a break; one medical issue after another! The hospital acted pretty quickly and indicated that they needed to carry out an operation under a local anaesthetic to remove the malignant cells. They would cut open a flap of skin, remove all the cells in the area and then sew back the flap over the top. It would be done as a day case, rather than having to stay in hospital overnight. They actually carried out the procedure on 10th May. It was a particularly stressful time for dad which was attested to by him having an angina episode the weekend before he was due to undergo the operation and later on the Monday morning after he had undergone the procedure. Fortunately, neither of them lasted for more than a few minutes.

Time was to prove that the operation had not necessarily cleared all the potentially harmful cells and he had to return for a further procedure about three months later to remove further cells. Thankfully, a final check-up towards the end of the year would indicate that he was clear of any further problem in this area.

Whilst we were waiting for the first operation Jacqueline had her 60th birthday. It actually fell on a Sunday and she decided that she would like us all to go out for a formal afternoon tea. There was a hotel we knew called The Runnymede-On-Thames, which had a lovely setting right on the River Thames near Egham – they did traditional full afternoon teas (finger sandwiches, scones and cakes). It was only about a twenty minute drive from Jacqueline's house, so was not too far to go. We all spent a leisurely afternoon there to mark Jacqueline's milestone.

It is interesting looking back at the photos of that day. Dad always looked younger than he was – probably partially because he did not go grey and kept a reasonable amount of his hair (I hope I follow suit) and also because he was always so articulate and knowledgeable in his conversations. People who didn't know him would always guess an age about ten years younger than he was. However, when I now look back at those photos they probably represent the first time that I really appreciated and acknowledged that he was looking old and increasingly frail (not surprising you will probably say given he was ninety two). That sort of acknowledgement though is never easy for a family member to come to terms with and accept. Particularly by a son or daughter regarding their father. He had always been my role model throughout life and to see this ageing and frailty was particularly difficult to accept. Often, as well, close family do not see such changes as clearly, as they see the person all the time – it is much easier to identify such changes when you only see a person every so often (snapshots at different points in time). That aspect would present some challenges over the next couple of years, as Jacqueline and I some-times came to acknowledge and accept permanent dete-riorations in dad's health and ability at different times.

On a brighter note, Jacqueline had been exploring the possibility of a longer cruise for dad if possible – as certain specific cruise lines and cruises apparently offered the possibility of carrying out dialysis on board (at a charge). Considering the positive response to the Norwegian Gem weekend back in 2007 she thought it would be something dad would really enjoy. An added restriction was that it would have to depart and return from the UK, as he was not able to fly given his medical condition. Eventually she found a specific Royal Caribbean trip departing from Southampton on 17th July returning two weeks later on 31st July. It was on the ship Independence of the Seas and would visit such places as Gibraltar, Nice, Pisa, Rome, Sardinia, Cadiz, Lisbon and Vigo. She decided that this time she would take dad away along with Andreas. Linda and I took a break instead for a week in June visiting our close friends, Chris and Marianne, in Bermuda.

The cruise was to be very much a curate's egg! For some reason, whether it was the changed routine, anxiety over a different dialysis facility or that it was simply too much at his age the first half of the cruise found dad quite unstable in terms of his angina. He had attacks on each of the first few days (sometimes in the early hours of the morning). Also Jacqueline had difficulty pinning the medical staff down to a regular dialysis schedule as he would have had at home – often this resulted in him dialysing at different times in the day, or on different days from normal (no doubt all of this contributed to an unstable condition/reaction of the body). Jacqueline and I were in contact most days and towards the end of the first week she was seriously thinking of requesting Royal Caribbean to "offload" them so they could get dad back to the UK. As it happens, things started to settle down slowly and the second week proved to be less traumatic and more stable (albeit he did have further angina episodes, including one on his last dialysis session on the Friday before the ship arrived back into Southampton on the Saturday morning). It certainly was anything but a relaxing holiday for Jacqueline!!

Having said that, they did manage to get off at various ports (sometimes Jacqueline would stay on board with dad, whilst Andreas wandered ashore). One was Pisa, where Jacqueline called me on her mobile phone from a café near where the leaning tower of Pisa was located – it was good to speak to her and dad and appreciate that there were some interesting and enjoyable parts of the trip. Linda and I had just taken a day trip to Pisa the previous month, for our wedding anniversary treat, so we could picture exactly where they were sitting when we got the phone call that day.

Jacqueline did get a short break over a weekend in Scotland, visiting some friends, later in August (after Andreas had spent some time back in Greece) and September saw us visiting Leeds again with dad for the usual catch up and visit to the cemetery. Throughout all this time Linda was still working full time and visiting her dad for one weekend a month – fortunately he had come to terms with the loss of Joyce better than I imagined and his health seemed to be holding up reasonably well (apart from a niggling hernia).

September brought about another medical issue (albeit not acute). Dad had been having increasing problems with his vision and it had been diagnosed as a cataract. He had previously undergone a cataract operation on the other eye in Leeds many years ago. Now it was time to do this one. Again, for speed and convenience, we arranged for this to be done privately. For those of you who have had any experience of such a procedure it is surprisingly quick. Normally, the actual operation only takes about half an hour with the eye numbed using anaesthetic drops. You are in and out of hospital within a few hours and fortunately everything went as planned for dad – having it done at the end of September. A follow-up appointment a couple of days later confirmed everything had gone okay. It was amazing when you look back that throughout the myriad of medical problems, procedures and operations, he never complained about his situation. He had an incredible resilience and positive attitude of mind. I think a lot of people of that generation display elements of those traits – more so than my generation. Whether it was the hardships and type of life they had, including dealing with a world war, I am not sure. In similar circumstances to dad I think I would have been complaining more and feeling much sorrier for myself!

It is around this time that I started to ruminate over a work decision. Similar to what had happened back in 2006, I could see the increasing frailty and problems engulfing dad. My ability to work full time and continue to provide the level of support I wanted to with Jacqueline was becoming a greater issue. Therefore, I decided to hand in my notice, albeit I was enjoying the work I was doing. As my official period of notice was three months I sat down with my Portfolio Director, Yvonne Mowlds, at the end of September and explained my position and thoughts. She was very understanding (as always) and said that although she/Monitor really didn't want to lose me, she fully understood the rationale and decision I had reached.

I really didn't give it any further thought until a couple of days later. Yvonne sat me down and floated an idea past me. She had been discussing the situation with the executive management and said there may be a "win-win" option to resolve the situation. She tabled the option of my moving to part time working (something that really didn't happen at Monitor at that time) – two or three days a week – carrying out a more project/development role in Compliance rather than the standard day-to-day Senior Relationship Manager position (with primary responsibility for twenty Foundation Trusts). I was taken aback and quite touched that she, in particular, and Monitor in general had bothered to expend the time and effort to create such an opportunity for me. After discussing this with Linda and Jacqueline I agreed to change over to two days a week from January 2011. We agreed on a default of my working Wednesday and Thursday, albeit some weeks we changed the days either for work or personal reasons – both sides were flexible in this respect. The change made a major difference in terms of always being able to be around when required for dad, yet still being able to continue to use my skills and experience to work. After all, even at this stage I was still only fifty six years old. For this I will always be extremely grateful and indebted to Yvonne.

As we moved into 2011 dad enjoyed his annual visit to the Panto at the New Victoria Theatre, Woking. A couple of days later was his first masonic lodge meeting of the year. Now that I was only working two days a week it made it easier for me to attend the lodge with him. Although my mother lodge was in London, I went along as dad's guest to each meeting. There was always a meal (festive board) held after the actual lodge meeting which lasted around an hour and a half. I think dad enjoyed this part of the evening as much as the ceremonial part, as it gave him the opportunity to socialise with all the other brethren. I always had somewhat mixed feelings at these get-togethers. It was good to be able to be there and share these experiences with dad, but the amount of support he needed just reminded me of how he was deteriorating over time. I often had to help him cut up some of his food, especially when he was having a flare up of his rheumatoid arthritis. We went to most of the monthly lodge meetings that year, unless he felt particularly unwell. Later on in the year I actually moved my membership to the lodge in Aldershot which made life somewhat easier. Dad struck up a good friendship with Michael Fenech, who happened to be the secretary of the lodge at the time. Over the coming years Michael would keep in contact and visit dad from time to time. He was also very supportive to Jacqueline and I during the latter part of dad's life and after his passing.

We were planning an early trip up to Leeds that year – in February. It had been an event that had been on the calendar for some time, subject to dad being well enough to travel. It was the coming of age ceremony (*"Barmitzvah"*) for Moira and David Gelman's son,

Jesse. This takes place in the Jewish religion when the boy reaches the age of thirteen. It would involve Jesse reading certain parts of the Saturday morning service in the synagogue and would then be followed by a celebratory, catered lunch for invited guests.

Just before that occasion, Jacqueline and Andreas had their wedding anniversary (6th February) and managed a weekend away in Brussels as a short break. I assumed "dad sitting" duties as normal.

Friday 18th February came around and after an earlier than normal dialysis session that day we set off for Leeds in the afternoon. This time we managed just to take my car, as Andreas decided to stay at home to do certain things he wanted to get finished. The one cloud hanging over the trip was that there was a forecast of snow over the weekend. For anyone who has tried to push a wheelchair in snow, believe me it is not easy! The rest of Friday went off as planned, but the snow started to come down after we reached the Holiday Inn at Garforth.

By the following morning it was already laid quite thick on the ground and continuing to come down. We made our way, gingerly, to the synagogue in North Leeds. The main road gates to the grounds of the synagogue were always closed on the Sabbath (as technically the most religious people would not be driving etc.). Despite finding the caretaker to the premises and explaining the mobility issue we had with dad and his age, he refused to open the locked gates (to my great irritation and exasperation). I manoeuvred the car as close as I could to the adjoining pedestrian entrance/path and we had to try and get dad out of the car and into the wheelchair in snow and slippery conditions.

After that, we had the challenge to get the wheelchair up the winding path and into the synagogue entrance. Not only were we all concerned about dad, but with it being particularly lethal underfoot I was equally as concerned as to Jacqueline and Linda's safety – the last thing we needed was one of them falling and breaking something. We could really have done with another pair of hands.

The ceremony and following reception/lunch went off well. It was quite rare now for dad to find himself in a synagogue and as a life president of another synagogue in Leeds he did enjoy taking part in such services. Although I seem to remember that the snow had actually stopped falling by the time we came out later that afternoon, it was still treacherous underfoot. I got Jacqueline and Linda to hold on tight to each of my arms as we walked carefully down the path to where I had brought the car around. I then wheeled dad down separately and we helped him back into the car. We all eventually got back to the hotel, having enjoyed the event, but heaving a sigh of relief that we were all back in one piece. Fortunately the thaw set in fairly quickly and by the time we set off on Sunday for the journey home the main roads were all quite reasonable.

In contrast to that weekend, Linda and I took a week off in March and had the pleasure of a Caribbean cruise with associated heat and sunshine. Towards the end of March Jacqueline managed a long weekend out in Greece with Andreas, who had gone out a few days before. However, the end of March brought a "near miss". Early one morning (around six o'clock) dad had a further angina episode. This took three sprays of GTN and about half an hour before the pain finally subsided – we were so close to another hospital admission on that occasion. Ironically, the next medical problem would concern me and not dad. One Friday morning in early May I was busy getting ready in the bathroom and bent down to dry my feet when all of a sudden I had a searing pain from my lower back. It travelled in slow motion down my right leg and right down into the big toe of that foot – I was in agony. A diagnosis would conclude that I had trapped the sciatic nerve. I spent most of the next couple of days flat out, only being able to get around on all fours (to stand upright was too painful). Fortunately with some strong muscle relaxants and painkillers from the GP and a couple of visits to my osteopath during the next fortnight, I managed to get back on an even keel. However, it did necessitate a long period of physiotherapy to get virtually all the movement and strength back in that leg and foot and I still have to do exercises every day to keep it from relapsing. It just shows you that doing the simplest, everyday thing can cause a problem in certain circumstances.

One plan that Jacqueline had been working on was to take dad away again for a long weekend to Paris – using the Eurostar. It would be just Friday to Sunday and so could fit in with his normal dialysis sessions at West Byfleet. Arrangements had been made to go on Friday 1st July but as always, fate took a hand at the last minute. The Monday beforehand dad started to suffer with stomach type pains again after he had dialysis earlier in the day!! By late evening we were all on our way to Frimley Park Hospital, having had to call an ambulance as his condition deteriorated. They admitted him and the likely diagnosis was ileitis (a chronic inflammation of the ileum – a portion of the small intestine). We had a real fear, given the long episode that dad had previously experienced in hospital and the fact that they had indicated that inflammation/infection could re-emerge at any time.

The mode of treatment was similar to last time in prescribing extremely strong antibiotics to try and eliminate any underlying cause. The only down side was that dad didn't tolerate strong antibiotics very well and they tended to knock him out, give him hallucinations etc., – but there was no viable alternative. Fortunately this time, the nurses moved dad into a side room, so he had his privacy, and allowed much more flexibility for Jacqueline and I to be there with him. He was obviously far more frail than he had been back in 2008 when he had his last long spell in hospital, so Jacqueline and I very quickly came to the conclusion that one of us needed to be there with him at all times. Not only did he need someone there to help him with any food we could get him to eat, but also to protect his fistula and ensure he received the correct medication all the time. Also, with the effects of the antibiotics on him, having someone familiar with him at all times was far more calming than coming to from time to time and not appreciating where he was or what was happening to him. Of the medical aspects, the fistula issue was always a major concern/fear. Despite all the notes/notices the nurses would make/put up, it was still very easy for someone to come along in the middle of the night to take his regular blood pressure, temperature etc., and go for the left arm (as the norm). There were times we had to stop that happening – so being there twenty four seven justified itself purely on those grounds.

Practical as ever, I drew up a schedule for Jacqueline and I so we could relieve each other at regular intervals.

That resulted in each of us spending some overnight sessions at his bedside. Trying to get some rest during the night sat in a normal chair, and putting your feet up on another one became a bit of a fine art! They were also quite lonely and reflective periods – it is natural for one's mind to turn back over all the events that had led to this point and to ponder on the possible outcomes and trials to come. Night time seems to have the inherent ability to trigger such reflections in the mind.

Again, work were very good with me as, at short notice, I took my two working days off as leave that week. Fortunately, dad started to respond to the antibiotics and we also managed to convince the West Byfleet centre to carry on dialysing him on the Wednesday and Friday that week – the last thing we needed was the trauma of having to get to and from St Helier's Hospital again; so far away. Yet another episode of "beating the odds" took place and Ian recovered enough to be discharged on Sunday 3rd July. Although reaching the decision to discharge was always a huge relief, there was always something in the back of my mind bringing dad home from the hospital that reminded me that, one day, we would not be so fortunate. It is something you are never prepared for, but have to try and acknowledge as a possibility that might need to be faced sooner rather than later.

One of the problems this latest spell in hospital had highlighted was the issue around respecting and communicating dad's wishes should he not be in a state to clearly communicate them at the time. The following year would see us having to address this in a more formal way through the courts, but in the interim we drew up a set of words that dad was happy with and he signed and dated it along with a non-family member witness (Moira Gelman in fact). It read:

"Until further notice I, Ian Miles Harris, of 29 Laird Court, Bagshot, Surrey, would like the following wishes to be taken into consideration should I not be in a position to clearly express these at the time required due to my medical condition.

(a) Should conservative treatment of my condition be proving ineffective/insufficient I would want any appropriate surgical procedure to be carried out – fully understanding the potential high risk of such a course of action, and
(b) Should the situation arise I would wish medical staff to make all attempts at resuscitation should it be required".

The second point was particularly crucial, as should dad's heart stop for any reason this made it clear that he wished for his resuscitation to be attempted (despite the possible consequences). Quite often with older, ill patients they agree to a DNR (Do Not Resuscitate) form being signed. Again it was a depressing topic that we would have to revisit during 2012.

That summer followed its usual pattern. We managed to take dad out some days when he felt up to it – to the local garden centre, where we often stopped off for a drink and cake, Birdworld, a trip down to the coast etc. The outings were becoming less frequent as the strain of dialysis (and other medical problems) inexorably took their physical toll – it was always an effort for him to go out, compared with something you and I would do without giving it much thought.

With the increasing back and hip discomfort we suggested to dad that he invested in a new, electric, adjustable bed. We felt that would give the added support by being able to be adjusted to the exact position he wanted (i.e. both the head end and for his legs). One of the suppliers of such orthopaedic beds came to discuss it with us and took various measurements so they could customise the bed as much as possible. Since the move from Leeds we had still been using the double bed he and mum used in the flat. The new bed arrived on a Monday morning (1st August). I think dad had mixed feelings at the time. Obviously he was anticipating the benefits from having the new bed, but seeing the bed that he and mum spent a number of years in being taken away must have been sad – another reminder of something lost. There were teething troubles as initially dad wasn't sure he was really comfortable in the new bed (exasperation on the part of Jacqueline and I), but eventually, with the appropriate mattress cover etc., he took to it. One of the practical benefits was that it created a lot more useable space in the bedroom – you could now get the wheelchair into the room and manoeuvre around without too much of a problem; it was easier to use the commode chair that was in the room as well. The extra space was to become essential over the coming year as things took their course.

Jacqueline managed a couple of short breaks to Greece over the summer – around four days at the end of August (including a couple of days on the island of Santorini) and then a long weekend later in September for a memorial service for one of Andreas's aunts – with me dad sitting as normal. In between we did manage the usual "annual" weekend in Leeds to visit the cemetery and friends – little did we know it at the time, but that would be his last visit back "home".

October saw Ian's ninety fourth birthday come and go – something I must admit we didn't believe we would see when this latest chapter in his life started back in 2006. He wasn't really up to a major party this year, but we all went over to The Compleat Angler in Marlow for formal afternoon tea, looking out over the Thames – a very pleasant afternoon. It was coincidence that David Gelman's birthday (Moira Gelman's husband) was also on 16th October – the same day as dad's birthday.

There had been fewer incidents of angina in 2011 than in 2010, but it remained a constant threat and worry. This was highlighted one Wednesday in November when dad had an episode around half past ten in the morning. Although it went off after a few minutes it always left him somewhat drained – not a good position to be in to have his dialysis later that day. He then had another attack just over an hour later. Considering the situation and possible cumulative effect, putting him through dialysis in the afternoon was probably not the best call. Jacqueline called the centre and explained the situation. As usual they were extremely helpful and said that in this instance they could actually move him back to Thursday and dialyse him then instead – which was an ideal solution in the circumstances. Although the dialysis sessions were still going reasonably well in general, considering the combination of the strain the procedure puts on the body and dad's low blood pressure it would not take much else to instigate a problem during dialysis (a risk none of us wished to take).

This was highlighted acutely at West Byfleet Dialysis Centre towards the end of the year. When we went to pick dad up one tea time it was immediately obvious that he had been quite shaken by something. It transpired that one of the ladies, opposite where dad's bed was, had died on dialysis that afternoon!! Obviously, the staff had made every attempt to resuscitate her (they have a defibrillator and an emergency crash cart on hand) and called an ambulance, but all to no avail. Despite them closing the curtains around her dialysis station, it had naturally shocked everyone. It certainly brought home the stresses dialysis placed on the body and the inherent dangers of undergoing the procedure. Dad was never really the same after that. Until then, he had been comfortable with us taking him in and picking him up after his session, but this latest incident really seemed to unsettle him and we started to actually stay with him throughout the sessions from then on.

December saw Jacqueline getting a long weekend away at the start of the month and then a few days between Christmas and New Year. Christmas followed the usual pattern, with me joining dad, Jacqueline and Andreas at Laird Court and Linda going down to Taunton to be with her dad and brother.

Ian & Fay Harris
Wedding 9th June 1948

Ruby Wedding Anniversary – 1988

Ian, Fay, Jacqueline & Russell
Golden Wedding Anniversary – 1998

Ian, Fay & Jacqueline
3 Cresta Court, Primley Park Garth, Leeds

Russell & Linda's Wedding – 17th June 2007

Graves of Ian & Fay Harris – Leeds

Chapter 7

There are always seminal moments in life that trigger an unstoppable chain of events. Sunday 15th January 2012 would provide one of those moments that would change all our lives dramatically over the following ten months (and leave their indelible mark forever).

During the previous year we had visits from occupational health staff who would advise on practical items that would make life easier at home for dad. One was a device that would allow him to have a bath as opposed to just a shower. Until then we used to put a seat in the bath and help dad over the high sides to get in. We would leave him to have his shower and then help him out afterwards. This new item was a seat-like device, but was electrically operated so that once he was sat down it could be lowered into the bath fully. Afterwards, we could use the handset to raise it fully upwards again and help him out. It worked well and dad seemed to appreciate it. However, there was one element none of us had thought about – the human factor.

It would normally be on a Sunday morning that dad had a bath – he had the time and also had recovered somewhat from the week's dialysis sessions. This particular Sunday started out as normal and Jacqueline helped dad get ready, into the bath and lowered him down. Normally he would give Jacqueline a call when he was finished and she would help him back out – but not this time. For some reason, he decided to try and get out himself. He had raised the seat as normal but had obviously slipped whilst trying to get out of the bath. Jacqueline thought he was taking a long time and called to him and then went back into the bathroom. There he was on the floor having fallen and hit his head on the adjacent toilet. It took both her and Andreas to haul him up onto the seat (there is not a lot of room to manoeuvre in a small bathroom). The immediate fear was that he might have broken something, but miraculously he seemed to have avoided that. Over the next few days he was very sore and tender and a lot of bruising came out. However, we all thought the same thing – we have really dodged a bullet there. Oh how wrong we were!

Life continued as normal for a few days until Jacqueline went to take dad down to the local hairdressers in Bagshot on Thursday 26th January. Suddenly, he said he was in agony with his back. The problem didn't subside over the weekend and we managed to get an appointment with his GP (Dr Johnson) on the Monday evening. The suggestion was that he arranged an appointment at Frimley Park for an overall review of dad's condition – this day assessment should include X-rays and any other scans necessary, plus a complete review of his condition (by a general consultant rather than a specialist for any particular aspect). Because of the extent of the pain and issues, the appointment actually took place just four days later on the Friday (necessitating moving dad's normal dialysis session to the Saturday afternoon instead). Those days saw dad in extreme pain, despite prescribed pain medication. Even with his electric, reclining armchair he couldn't find a position to relieve the pain, even with the support of pillows etc. Also trying to get him up and down stairs, albeit using the wheelchair and stair lift, was a major challenge needing a lot of support from two people.

Our hopes were pinned on the Friday assessment, in terms of a positive diagnosis and proposed action plan, but they were dashed by a pretty shambolic day. The assessments were not as thorough or extensive as we had been led to believe. Also, the amount of time taken and waiting around was extensive, just adding to dad's already severe discomfort. At one point we had to insist that they found him some sort of bed to lie down on, as sitting normally or in the wheelchair was becoming untenable. They eventually sorted out a makeshift bed so he could lie flat and alleviate some of the pain. Finally, an X-ray was taken of dad's back, but then they didn't have an orthopaedic specialist to review it – so again, another substantial wait until a specialist working in the Accident & Emergency department at the time could take time out to have a look at it. Eventually the assessment came back that there were no breakages in the back as far as they could ascertain – this was to prove to be an inaccurate diagnosis!

This unhelpful day was followed by a further CT scan of dad's head on the following Tuesday afternoon (due to the fact that he had hit it during the fall). Getting the results of this procedure seemed to take a number of days, as again it needed to await the review of a neurosurgeon at St George's Hospital. Eventually we managed to extract the feedback. We were simply told that there was "no intervention necessary". In hindsight maybe we should have pushed for a more detailed explanation of this feedback. We were obviously pleased that there was nothing to be done in this respect (as we had our hands full with the other physical problems dad was experiencing), but probing more deeply might have unearthed a fuller explanation. From what transpired over the following months, in terms of the decline of his mental ability, it became clear that there must have been some damage caused by the fall, but that the specialist's view was obviously that there was little that could be done given his overall condition.

After the unhelpful assessment day we decided to pursue a private path in terms of ascertaining what the problem (and possible solution) was to dad's pain. A private consultation was arranged with Lt. Col. McErlain, a consultant orthopaedic surgeon, on Wednesday 8th February at Spire Clare Park Hospital at Farnham. The journey would take about forty to forty five minutes from Bagshot. We decided that to try and minimise dad's pain we would engage a private ambulance again to take us there. After the appointment we would have to take him directly over to the dialysis centre for his usual session, so minimising the discomfort in one direction was the least we could do.

Mr McErlain was excellent and carried out a very thorough examination and assessment. He suspected there may be a breakage, but needed an MRI scan to be able to confirm this hypothesis. He arranged for this to take place the following morning at Frimley Park Hospital (where he also worked as part of the NHS). He also arranged for us to obtain a back brace from Frimley Park that might help alleviate some of the discomfort by providing additional support to the back and prescribed some Morphine patches to help with the pain. This was in addition to the Tramadol medication that had been prescribed after the assessment day the previous Friday.

A follow up appointment with Mr McErlain took place at Frimley Park that Friday and our worst fears were confirmed. There had been a fracture of the L1 vertebrae in dad's lower back. In normal circumstances this might have gradually repaired itself, but would take at least a couple of months. However, it may also go the other way and start to collapse further. In such circumstances the standard approach would be to undertake a relatively short operation to inject "cement" into the break to bolster the area and alleviate a lot of the pain. He proposed we had a further X-ray done in two weeks' time and depending on whether it was improving or deteriorating, make a further decision then. Linda and I had already arranged a week away on holiday later in February, but cancelled all plans as it was obvious this situation was not going to resolve itself in the short term.

We had some support from a District Nurse who came in on a regular basis to help with the situation. However, it soon became clear that we were not going to get through another couple of weeks or so before going back to the hospital – as matters were getting worse rather than better. We were also starting to witness more angina episodes, which was not surprising considering the mental and physical stress dad was going through.

Getting to and from dialysis was becoming a major exercise as well. We had hit on the idea of arranging for a wheelchair taxi to take us both ways rather than using our cars – this reduced the number of times dad had to get into and out of a wheelchair, so as to minimise the pain. Instead of getting out to get into a car and the opposite at the dialysis centre, we could just push the wheelchair into the taxi and out again at the other end. We ended up using the same person – Mr Shah – on a regular basis. He was extremely under-standing and flexible in terms of these trips, visits to the hospital etc. He was also extremely careful in the way that he drove to ensure that there was as few bumps and discomfort to dad as possible. It is a reflection that throughout all the difficulties we encountered over the years, when you really need help and understanding it is heart-warming as to how many people actually "step up to the plate" and provide it.

Talking about mobility, we had been given some advice and help from local nurses in terms of moving dad both on his dialysis bed and at home. For mobility difficulties nurses often use a "slide sheet" to make things easier for all concerned. A slide sheet is made of very low friction material and is a continuous item (like a fan belt; escalator etc.,) just a bit wider than a person. You slightly roll the person from each side to get the sheet under them and then with one person on each side you grab the sheet and slide it in one direction moving the patient on top accordingly. This is great for moving a patient up a bed or chair when they have slipped down (without having to grab and pull them directly). We had been given such a sheet which proved invaluable as time went on.

One example of its use was an evening after we had brought dad back from dialysis. We got him settled in his electric reclining chair where he normally had a sleep after the exertions of the dialysis session. I left for home, but not long afterwards I got a call from

Jacqueline. With the chair reasonably reclined dad had somehow slipped down so that his bottom was on the elevated leg rest rather than still on the chair. He no longer had the ability to move himself back up and Jacqueline couldn't manage it on her own (Andreas didn't happen to be around). If she electrically moved the chair into the upright position the footrest would go down and dad would end up on the floor! I made my way back to Laird Court and after some consideration we came to the conclusion that using the slide sheet would probably be the only safe and practical way to get him back upright. Fortunately, with a bit of adaptation and effort we managed to succeed and slid the sheet (and dad) back up into the chair. Although it was just another of the challenges that Jacqueline and I dealt with, dad was quite upset at the situation. In hindsight, I think it was as much the realisation and confirmation of how he had deteriorated and how limited in movement and dependent he had become, as it was the particular embarrassment of getting himself into that position. As usual, Jacqueline and I just tried to make light of it saying it was just one of those things – no problem.

We were back at Frimley Park seeing Mr McErlain on Tuesday 21st February. He agreed that the surgical team would go ahead with the operation sooner rather than later – he could carry it out himself on 29th February or one of his colleagues may perform the operation sooner if a slot became available. He felt that under the circumstances they would try to perform the procedure (technically called vertebroplasty) under a local anaesthetic along with a general relaxant. It would mean coming in one day for the procedure with the preference being for an overnight stay and (all being well) he could be discharged the following day in order that he could attend dialysis. This wasn't the easiest of procedures and there was a reasonable element of risk associated with it. Also, even if initially successful, there could then be some wear on adjacent vertebrae due to the stiffness of the cemented joint. In reality though we could not go on the way we were and all agreed to go ahead as soon as possible. As it happens, a slot was available just a couple of days later with Mr Chatakondu (the senior consultant surgeon) available to perform the procedure – so Thursday 23rd February it was.

The dialysis session on the Wednesday wasn't a good prequel for the operation the next day. Dad had an angina episode whilst on the machine and needed a couple of GTN sprays to alleviate the condition. Thursday 23rd was a very early start as we needed to be at Frimley Park for seven o'clock in the morning to book in. There was some issue in finding a bed initially after we booked in, but after a pre-operation examination they allocated a room in the private wing of the hospital, Parkside (probably because vacant beds were in short supply elsewhere at that time). We eventually got dad settled in there and into bed and awaited the surgeon and anaesthetist to come and discuss the proposed procedure with us. It was likely that the operation would not take place until early that afternoon, given the list of patients due to be operated on that day.

We had a visit from two or three of the surgical team during the morning and there was an unexpected change of tack. Due to the exact nature of the break it was not going to be possible to carry out the surgery using a local anaesthetic as originally indicated. Also, the normal approach would be to have the patient lying face down on the operating table, to make it straight forward to access the area of the back required – but with dad's condition such a position would be quite dangerous in terms of possible breathing/heart complications. The general anaesthetic approach brought a whole new dimension to the situation we all faced – the risks associated with the operation had just gone up exponentially. We all had long conversations with the team involved and the bottom line was this – Mr Chatakondu was prepared to attempt the procedure, but the expert opinion was that the odds of survival (considering the general anaesthetic etc.,) were only about 50:50 – the choice was ours (or Ian's to be more precise)!! They left the three of us to have a serious conversation about how we would like to proceed. What followed was one of the most difficult conversations Jacqueline and I had ever had to have with dad.

Jacqueline and I were sat either side of the bed and we started to go through and summarise the situation for dad as best we could – setting out the pros and cons of proceeding with the operation or not. We were trying to keep as calm and objective as we could, but we were quite clear of the enormity of the decision to be made. We both realised that logically there was no alternative but to proceed with the operation despite the level of risk – dad would have no quality of life and would continue to suffer in extreme pain if something wasn't done. However, our hearts new that there was an equal risk that we could be leaving the hospital later that day without a father! Dad's initial reaction was that he didn't think he wanted to go ahead given the circumstances. We fully understood why this should be his first reaction – if someone is basically saying there is an equal chance of you dying on the operating table to surviving, everyone's survival instinct would be to say thanks, but no thanks. Jacqueline and I looked across the bed at each other. Nothing was said, but we were of one thought – there really isn't an alternative; dad needed to go ahead with the operation. I don't know how long it was that we continued the conversation and discussion between the three of us – it seemed like an eternity, but in reality was probably just a few minutes. Maybe it was the initial shock subsiding and/or dad's logical side kicking in (he was always an extremely logical and practical/pragmatic person) but eventually he gradually came round to the conclusion that if that was the only realistic way to improve his condition then he would agree to go ahead with it.

Such times always leave you with self-questioning and doubt afterwards. You tend to question whether your conclusion as to the best way forward was purely due to it being the best option for the person concerned, or a way to alleviate your own stress in dealing with the ongoing situation. On reflection, in this case, the decision was congruent in (hopefully) benefitting all parties involved; albeit to this day I am convinced that the primary driver for Jacqueline and I was that something desperately needed to be done to alleviate dad's pain and suffering.

We communicated the decision to the medical staff and they proceeded with the paperwork accordingly – dad needed to sign a consent form acknowledging the risks involved. After that it was a waiting game until they came to take him down to the operating theatre. Eventually the door opened and the staff said they were ready to take him down to theatre. We asked if we could come down with dad as far as the entrance and they said certainly. In some ways that walk was akin to the death row walk of a condemned prisoner – wondering whether there would be a last minute reprieve. We entered the outer preparation room to the theatre and the staff indicated that we now needed to leave. In turn both Jacqueline and I leant over and kissed dad and said "I love you" and that we would see him soon. As he disappeared into the theatre and we went back into the corridor Jacqueline broke down and sobbed and we just held each other, with tears rolling down my face – was that the last time we would touch, speak to and see dad alive?

We slowly made our way back up to the reception/waiting area of the Parkside suite. Like all these situations time seemed to almost stand still. I seemed to recall that we had a drink and were flicking through magazines etc., – to be honest my mind was not clear given the circumstances. We had been given an indication of how long the procedure would take. That time came and went, as did a further quarter of an hour, then half an hour and still no news. My heart was starting to sink (as I didn't interpret this elongation of the timescale as a good indication) and I was starting to try and steel myself to receive the worst communication possible. Eventually I did pluck up the courage to go and talk to the staff on reception (although I wasn't sure I really wanted to hear their answer), who said they would follow up and see if they could ascertain any news for us. Again, more minutes went by in silence. Finally one of the reception staff came over and I held my breath – then she said that apparently dad had come through the operation and we could wander down to the recovery room to see him in a few minutes. The relief was unbelievable and palpable – he had done it yet again; beaten the odds!

Despite the fact that we didn't know how successful the operation would prove to be, we walked down to the recovery room as if a tonne weight had been lifted from us. The recovery room is not dissimilar from an Accident & Emergency department – with a number of beds separated by curtains. Once the staff are satisfied that the patient is stable they would then be taken back to a normal ward. We spent a while with dad, talked and gave him a drink of water. Once they were happy that his vital signs were satisfactory and that the main effects of the anaesthetic had worn off, they moved him back onto one of the main wards. The idea was that he would stay in overnight and that, subject to everything being alright, they would discharge him the next day (Friday) so he could attend dialysis at West Byfleet in the afternoon. A little while later Mr Chatakondu came up to the ward to talk to us all. He explained what he had to do in theatre and that it was one of the trickiest operations he had had to perform – he said that at one point he had to have staff hold dad up on an incline so that he could complete the operation. He also joked that his hair had probably turned a further shade of grey today due to the stress levels! We thanked him profusely and he said that, all being well, he would see us in clinic in about three weeks' time when they would do a further x-ray to ensure everything was satisfactory.

The following day a couple of nurses from the physiotherapy department who specialised in orthopaedics came up to the ward to test out the situation. They helped Ian get out of bed and using a Zimmer frame asked him to walk half way up and down the ward. This was the real moment of truth as prior to the operation dad couldn't even stand properly, let alone walk anywhere. He suddenly started to shuffle along using the Zimmer fame – it seemed almost like a miracle. The only down side was that Jacqueline and I had a difference of opinion with the nurses. We obviously knew how limited his walking capabilities had become even before the fall and the nurses were not cognisant of this and so were using their standard rule of thumb in terms of the distance they wanted him to walk before they were happy to recommend a discharge. There were some heated words between us as we were concerned that they would push Ian too far too soon – and then we might have collateral consequences when he needed to go for dialysis that afternoon. Anyway, he did manage to go half way up the ward and back – probably a combination of the improvement due to the operation and sheer dogged determination to get out of hospital! The outcome was positive – yes, he could go home.

Fortunately, the dialysis went off without incident that afternoon. Whether it was the after effects of everything that had happened the last few days, or just the increasing trend of angina episodes, there were another couple of short angina attacks on that Sunday afternoon and then Monday morning. It would transpire that he would have over twenty such episodes during 2012 – more than double the number experienced the previous year.

Around this time we had been discussing getting in some further support an odd afternoon a week when I was at work (I was still working part time – two days a week), which would provide some alleviation for Jacqueline. Over time it would work out that Bart, who had built up such a good friendship with dad at dialysis, had the capacity to help us all out. This would provide the further support for us that would prove beneficial and also a welcome change for dad on a social level, albeit this support did not kick in on a regular basis for a few weeks.

The early indications were that the back operation had been successful. There seemed to be a dramatic reduction in the pain initially after coming home, but unfortunately the benefit would not last and within a couple of weeks the pain level was again reaching a significant level. Monday 12th March saw dad switching to an early dialysis session in order that we could go back for the outpatients appointment with Mr Chatakondu in the afternoon. His examination and the associated x-ray did not result in good news. Although the actual operation on the vertebrae had been successful, the lower area of dad's back was deteriorating. As previously mentioned, he had been having some problems over recent years in that respect, but obviously the fall had exacerbated the damage and deterioration. We were now moving into a different phase with this problem. It would no longer be possible to propose any further treatment that would reverse or rectify the fundamental problem. The only avenue now left open was to minimise the pain and discomfort as far as possible.

The initial recommendation by Mr Chatakondu was for Ian to have facet joint injections into the lower back which may help to alleviate the pain (at least for a period of time). This could be done as a day case with just a local anaesthetic and so would pose minimal risk.

This would bring us in contact with the pain management team at Frimley Park, who like most of the staff there, proved to be extremely helpful and supportive. The procedure was scheduled in for Saturday 31st March.

After the outpatients visit there was also the regular session with Dr Marsh, dad's renal doctor, at West Byfleet the following morning. This was a regular clinic each renal patient attended every few weeks and was held at the West Byfleet centre in the upstairs facilities. At least the timing of this appointment allowed us to bring Dr Marsh up to date, first hand, with everything that had been happening at Frimley over the previous weeks. We would end up working very closely with Dr Marsh over the following months.

After the vertebroplasty operation had initially seemed to be successful, I had resurrected our (shortened) plans to have a few days break in the sun a couple of weeks later. However, it was not to be. Not only did the pain start to return but also during the week commencing 19th March there was another visit to Frimley Park Accident & Emergency department due to a more extensive angina attack. In the circumstances I had no option but to cancel the break yet again at the last minute. The "roller coaster" ride of hopes and fears was bucking and twisting as it would continue to do for some time.

On 31st March Mr Shah took us in to Frimley Park hospital in the taxi as normal. We needed to be there by eleven o'clock so at least it was a more civilised time for dad rather than seven a.m. when he had gone in for his back operation. We settled in to the day case ward and they checked and prepared dad accordingly. They were to administer a set of injections on either side of the L3, L4 and L5 vertebrae in the lower back area. The hope was that these would help alleviate a lot of the pain – at least for a period. Again, there was no saying they would work, or if they did, how long the relief would last. If they did work for a reasonable length of time, it would be possible to repeat the procedure at certain intervals.

The procedure went off without a problem and we were cleared to take dad home around twelve o'clock – again we called Mr Shah who dropped by to pick us up. It was a case of crossing fingers and hoping this latest approach would have the desired effect. We were finding that due to his extreme discomfort dad would often resort to going to bed rather than staying downstairs in his armchair, as laying fairly flat relieved the pressure on the spine and proved to be a lot more comfortable. Like everything, there happened to be a downside to this as well – if people lie in bed for extended periods there is a major risk of developing pressure sores on their back, heels etc., (despite taking appropriate precautions). He was also having discomfort with one of his toes which had turned black and did not look to be in a good condition. This was probably damaged during the fall as well. We ensured the district nurses kept a close eye on this, but there wasn't a lot specifically we could do but to leave well alone and hope it started to heal itself.

At this point only a couple of months had passed since the major problems flared up towards the end of January, yet in many ways it felt like years. The intensity of the 24/7 problems, the never ending round of appointments, procedures, angina episodes etc., were extremely draining for all of us. Faced with such circumstances, there are times when you just want to run away from it all. That's a natural reaction as emotionally you just want to get yourself out of what was proving to be a nightmare – it probably harks back to the intrinsic "fight or flight" instinct humans used to have. However, for most people that is just not an option and the other emotion of desperately wanting to help a loved one who is in pain and distress, is far more overwhelming. After a while you do become quite blinkered and short-term in approach in just focussing on dealing with the challenges of the next few hours or days rather than anything longer term. Little did we appreciate that this was still the early stages in what would prove to be an elongated dark period in our lives.

The next month was a lot more of the same. Although the facet joint injections did have some benefit it wasn't long before we realised this was only going to be a short term relief and the level of pain started to build again. He was also having to endure a couple of pressure sores, despite trying to take all steps to avoid these occurring. A particularly bad one was on the heel of one foot and despite all the help and dressings provided by the district nurses, it was proving to be very stubborn in healing. No doubt this was being compounded by the poor state of dad's body generally, so any healing was difficult.

A return appointment at the hospital on the last day in April didn't provide any good news either. It was clear by then that the facet joint injections would not provide any reasonable solution. Anyone seeing dad slumped in his wheelchair at that out-patients clinic, with the obvious pain written all over his face would have concluded the same thing. The last real throw of the dice was now to administer a caudal epidural injection into the back to try and kill as much pain as possible – again something that could be carried out as an out-patient on the day case ward. Due to dad's extreme condition they scheduled this just four days later on Friday 4th May.

It was a feeling of déjà vu early that Friday morning as we were back on the day case ward. The timing was earlier in the day than our previous visit so that dad could proceed with his normal dialysis session in the afternoon. However, the pre procedure examination of dad threw up a further problem (yet again). There was a pressure sore exactly where the doctors would normally have given the injection – sods law! In the circumstances they decided to give two injections, one from either side of the intended site, to try and achieve the same outcome. The procedure took place as planned and fortunately the afternoon session at dialysis didn't throw up any further dramas. Again it would be a case of wait and see in terms of the efficacy of the epidural.

It had been Jacqueline's sixty second birthday in the middle of that week – albeit there had been no real opportunity for celebration given the circumstances. However, on the Saturday Linda and I "dad sat" that afternoon and evening, so Jacqueline could have some sort of break and birthday celebration out. As I have reflected earlier in this book, when faced with such situations you have to cling on to every opportunity for a break from the nightmare – even if it is just a few hours where you relinquish primary responsibility for a person's care.

Jacqueline's birthday had also brought into focus another major aspect of dad's deterioration – his mental state. Although his communication had deteriorated over the previous weeks, with conversations being generally much shorter in nature (down to a few words) and less frequent, the extent of the deterioration was highlighted by an event related to Jacqueline's birthday. I had bought a birthday card for dad to give to Jacqueline and one afternoon, whilst she was out of the room, I sat down with dad so he could write/sign the card. It rapidly became obvious that he was finding great difficulty both framing the words to write and actually being able to write them. In the end I suggested some words and also that I would write them on the card and he could sign it – which he proceeded to do with some difficulty. I popped it in its envelope and then passed it back to him to write "To Jacqueline" on the front (as he always did). To my dismay he couldn't remember how to spell Jacqueline's name correctly!! With some help we finally got there, but it was one of the heart breaking moments for me in this whole journey to date. To see this wonderful, intelligent and articulate man reduced to this was a crime. At that moment I started to understand how people feel when caring for those with dementia and other similar diseases – but in this case the cause had probably been mainly due to the blow on the head when he fell in January.

Again, the next few days proved that although the epidural injections had some beneficial effect this was unlikely to last for any length of time, nor alleviate the pain to a reasonably tolerable level. Amazingly, we did have a chance to get dad out one weekend in the middle of May for a couple of hours to the local garden centre, Longacres. It was a place we had been many times and spent enjoyable afternoons/sitting and having a drink and cake in their café. We were trying to give dad some stimulation and change in the middle of the appalling circumstances we found ourselves in. We did go into the café, which had recently been refurbished and ordered some drinks, but this was a sad rather than enjoyable occasion. I still retain the imprint in my memory of looking across the table at dad crumpled in his wheel-chair, eyes half closed trying to deal with the constant pain. That picture would haunt me for some time after he was gone, whenever Linda and I dropped in to the café at Longacres. I am not one hundred percent sure, but I think that was the last time we ever had the oppor-tunity to take dad out (apart from the necessities of hospital and dialysis appointments).

The rest of May was interspersed with a couple of hospital visits – one for a cortisone injection into dad's hip for problems there and a follow up appointment with Mr McErlain generally about his back and condi-tion. At the latter one there was a basic admission that there really wasn't any further procedure they had at their disposal to help dad and that the way forward would be to try and ascertain the best way to try and minimise the level of pain. To this end we followed up with discussions with the specialist Pain Management Team at Frimley Park. As always, they were extremely helpful and gave as good advice as possible including what oral pain relief to administer etc., – including Fentanyl patches (slow release pain relief) and Amitriptylene (a nerve pain killer and anti-depressant).

However, we realised that we had pretty well reached the end of the road in terms of help that the hospital could provide and we arranged a session with Dr Johnson – dad's GP – for Monday 28th May at 11:20

a.m. to talk through what we should do from that point forward, as Jacqueline and I were now moving into unknown territory as to how to deal with the situation on an ongoing basis (or what support/options were available). This had been highlighted by an incident that occurred between Jacqueline and I just prior to that. It happened one evening at Laird Court when we needed to get dad from the living room back up to bed. There was just the two of us as I seem to recall Andreas was out in Greece. Although we were using the wheel-chair to move dad from his armchair to the stair lift, getting on to the chair lift necessitated helping him to stand and then turn around to sit on the stair lift. This was extremely difficult given the limited space available and the fact that he couldn't really support himself and was effectively a "dead weight".

Most times this manoeuvre was difficult, but that evening we seemed to be struggling more than ever. At that moment I suddenly realised that this situation wasn't sustainable (especially as Jacqueline had prob-lems with her back as well) – we simply couldn't carry on trying to do this day after day, week after week and I snapped and said so out loud to Jacqueline. It was probably the cumulative stress over the preceding months and the strain of that particular moment but she didn't react well and in no time we were shouting at each other. At one point I felt she was almost becoming hysterical so (stupidly) slapped her face lightly to try and bring her back to reality – all that did was to make her worse and she lashed out at me scratching my face just under the eye. It ended up by her shouting for me to get out and that she would deal with it all herself. Despite seeing red and wanting to say "fine" and storm out I realised I simply could not do that. In his current state it would be impossible for one person to handle dad and get him upstairs and into bed – and at the end of the day that was the only objective – so I stayed and we eventually managed to get him there.

In hindsight, this outburst was probably one of the worst and one of the best things that happened. I still feel guilty to this day for what transpired and particularly because this was all right in front of dad – I am sure he was so hurt by seeing his two children fighting like this and he would probably have blamed himself, because he would have felt that it was only happening because of him and his condition. I should have had this conversation (and argument if necessary) AFTER we had got dad upstairs, not during – but stress comes out in illogical ways at times. On the other hand, I think it may have focussed both of us on moving forward in looking at what help might be needed on an ongoing basis.

Linda and I managed a short three day break at the end of May and Bart came to assist Jacqueline one afternoon during that time. We arrived back for the session with the GP on the Monday morning.

The session with Dr Johnson was not a comfortable one. He went through the full range of problems dad was suffering from, including the issues of pressure sores, his mental state etc., – as well as all the procedures that had taken place over the previous months. He examined him as best he could, but obviously dad couldn't now even stand without complete support. He tried to talk to dad and discuss matters with him, but the responses were minimal (albeit I think he understood most of what was being said to him – he just found it difficult to respond or express himself at the time).

Dr Johnson's conclusion was that we were moving into a situation where we needed to consider palliative care ("end of life services" as he referred to them) and what elements would be appropriate and beneficial for dad. The key would be to minimise pain and distress and also specifically to try and address the pressure sores that were currently causing so much discomfort. In terms of the latter he said he would arrange for a nurse to visit who was a specialist in terms of tissue viability – she would be able to determine the best approach and provide support and guidance as necessary. In terms of the general palliative care he explained that this would be co-ordinated through a lady called Sarah Ivy. She was based at Woking Hospice, but was responsible for co-ordinating all aspects of palliative care for people wishing to remain at home – she would interface with GPs, district and palliative care nurses (e.g. the Beacon nurses in our area) and any providers of equipment such as beds, mattresses etc. Dr Johnson did push Jacqueline and I very hard in terms of our wish to keep dad at home. From his years of experience he obviously appreciated the extent of the commitment and stress this would place on the family as opposed to agreeing a move to a hospital or care home – however, Jacqueline and I were adamant that we wanted him to remain at home.

Dr Johnson would also liaise with dad's renal doctor – Dr Marsh. Apart from bringing him up to speed on the situation, he said he would need to understand what Dr Marsh felt was the best approach in terms of dialysis – whether that should continue, be reduced or stopped. The latter point sent a chill down our spines as we fully appreciated that if dialysis was stopped then the time left would be very short! Also, we had reached the situation where dad would really need ambulance transport to and from dialysis going forward (if it continued) as even using a wheelchair taxi was now presenting major problems. We all left the surgery somewhat stunned. Obviously, thoughts of when the end might come had been in the back of our minds for a number of years, but despite dad beating the odds on so many occasions the inevitable was catching up with us – we were entering that final phase. It was a numbing experience to come to terms with.

Arrangements were made for Sarah Ivy to visit the house that Saturday afternoon, but before that I put in a call to Dr Marsh myself. Jacqueline and I wanted to understand what the implications would be if dialysis was reduced, or became infeasible to continue – what would dad (and we) be faced with practically? Dr Marsh was as empathetic and helpful as always. We had quite a lengthy, sombre conversation around the subject. We discussed what generally happened physically when a person stopped receiving dialysis. This was not as traumatic as I had been fearing. My mind had been thinking back to dad's condition just prior to him being diagnosed with renal failure back in 2006 – and all the angina attacks. Dr Marsh indicated that what was far more likely to happen was a gradual weakening of the body, with the person sleeping more and more, lack of food intake etc., until they finally passed away. He indicated that the timescale would normal be one to two weeks after dialysis ceased. He said in the circumstances that he would authorise ambulance transport from now on for dad, which would minimise the distress of dialysis days. He also wished to have a session with us all prior to dad's dialysis session on 11th June, so he could assess the situation in detail, talk through the options and make the optimum decision regarding treatment going forward. The session would also include a specialist dialysis nurse, Jackie McNicholas.

One question we did discuss was my trepidation concerning *who* would decide that the time had come to stop the dialysis – would we be having to make such a decision. Again, Dr Marsh was re-assuring. He indicated that in virtually all such cases the situation itself determined the decision in terms of reaching a point where the patient simply was not well enough to tolerate further dialysis.

Changes took place pretty quickly in the next few days. A specialist bed and mattress were now required by dad as he was effectively bed bound. This would be needed by him in terms of maximising comfort and minimising the bed sores as well as being appropriate for the district nurses etc., that would visit – it needed to be adjustable for height, have side rails if needed and the mattress could be controlled electrically for various levels of firmness and other settings. We anticipated it looking like a stark hospital bed, but in fact aesthetically it was quite reasonable. Unfortunately, the lovely, custom made adjustable bed that dad had bought less than a year ago had to be dismantled and confined to the garage.

The other piece of essential equipment was a type of turntable. Even managing to get dad to stand upright out of bed, his ability to turn and move around was virtually non-existent. This piece of metal equipment had a handle at the top of a central pole, with the pole welded to a circular base which had the ability to turn on the floor/carpet. If we could help dad sit on the side of the bed and then stand upright onto the circular plate (holding the vertical handle) we could then just turn the plate and move him around. This proved to be essential, firstly to get out of bed for dialysis and secondly so he could use the commode chair which we had in the bedroom. The commode chair was something we had brought down from Leeds and was excellent. Under normal circumstances it just looked like a steel framed chair with a grey padded seat and two arms with padding thereon. However, the seat could be lifted off to reveal a bowl below for use as a commode.

As he had promised, Dr Marsh arranged for ambulance transport to be provided from now on to take dad to and from the West Byfleet centre. Normal patient transport was contracted with a company called GSL, but for dad they were using a small private ambulance company. It was owned and run by a first rate guy called Graham (and his wife) and normally the two staff who transported dad were a young lady called Donna and an older man called Steve. Sometimes Graham himself (or his son) would come instead dependent upon what their commitments were. They were excellent with dad and we all built up a close friendship over the coming weeks.

The journeys and dialysis were still traumatic for dad. We all did everything possible to make him as comfortable as we could, but there was no getting away from the fundamental condition he was in. We had a foam mattress which we always put underneath him when he was laid on the ambulance bed and then transferred that across to his bed at the dialysis centre when we arrived there. There were special "V" pillows we used and other blankets etc. In order to get him from the bedroom to the ambulance this necessitated most of us giving a hand and working together. We worked out a technique for him to roll onto his side in bed and then sit upright (like a pendulum) on the edge of the bed. We would then put his dressing gown on over the top of his pyjamas (it was no longer feasible to get him dressed) and then supported him as he got hold of the turntable equipment and stood up/held on. We would then turn it around and Donna and Steve would hold him and lower him into a transportable chair that they carried with them. They would then cover him up in a blanket and strap him in, so they could lift the chair and carry it downstairs and out into the ambulance. Once in the ambulance, again we would all help lift him onto the bed prepared with the foam mattress on. This necessitated one of the crew holding dad under his arms, the other getting ready to lift his legs and Jacqueline or I putting our hands under his lower back/bottom and we would all lift him simultaneously onto the bed!

This whole transfer procedure became increasingly painful and upsetting for dad as the weeks went on. Quite often he would be reduced to tears just by the procedure of getting him from the bed into the transportable chair in the bedroom. Seeing someone who had been so strong in our lives reduced to tears in this way on a regular basis was awful for Jacqueline and I to experience.

The transfer at the Dialysis Centre was easier as the crew simply rolled the ambulance bed to the side of his dialysis bed, ensured it was at the same height and then we would all take a corner of the foam mattress under him and slide it (and dad) across onto the dialysis bed.

Coming back everything worked in reverse, except back in the bedroom the transportable chair was too low for dad to stand up from, so we all ended up lifting him from there onto the bed manually (like we did in the ambulance going to dialysis). The dialysis sessions themselves were not straight forward, but I will return to that topic later.

Also around this time, we were prescribed something called Oxynorm for dad to help with the pain. This came in liquid form and was administered orally, a few millilitres at a time as required. It contained the active ingredient oxycodone hydrochloride, which is a type of medicine called an opioid painkiller. It is related to morphine. Opioid painkillers work by mimicking the action of naturally occurring pain-reducing chemicals called endorphins. Endorphins are found in the brain and spinal cord and reduce pain by combining with opioid receptors. They block the transmission of pain signals sent by the nerves to the brain. Therefore, even though the cause of the pain may remain, less pain is actually felt.

Saturday 2nd June came around and we sat down with Sarah Ivy in the living room at Laird Court to discuss the whole situation. As well as Jacqueline and I, Andreas happened to be around at the time, having returned from Greece on the previous Monday, so Jacqueline ensured he joined us in the discussions that followed. It was a somewhat surreal experience in some ways. Although emotions were obviously running at a high level we both needed to be as practical in this con-versation as possible, exploring all the implications surrounding keeping dad at home and all the avenues we might find ourselves being taken down. In this way we would be best equipped to deal with whatever was to come.

We went through all the day to day aspects such as the visits we could expect from the district nurses to deal with general matters of pain, bed sores, help with washing if required etc.; the specialist Beacon nurses in terms of additional support and what they would provide (initially Sarah could offer two nights a week of their time to sit with dad overnight and thus allow Jacqueline some better nights of sleep); medication both in the current situation and to cover other possible deteriorating conditions. Sarah recommended that she arrange the delivery of a slow release injection pump (like they use in hospital) and a set of sealed vials of various painkilling and other drugs, so that should dad urgently need to be administered such items, or have a slow release injection set up intravenously, it could be done immediately by one of the nurses (day or night) – rather than having to authorise/obtain all of the equipment and drugs at the time.

The other painful subject discussed was that of resuscitation should dad have heart failure. Until now we had always said yes to this (as was dad's wishes), but his condition was now dramatically different. From Sarah explaining the practicalities and possible effects of trying to resuscitate someone we realised that given we were in an end of life period anyway, proceeding with a resuscitation (should the situation arise) would simply prolong the agony for dad even further. After much soul searching we agreed that a *"Do not attempt cardiopulmonary resuscitation"* form should be completed and authorised by the medical staff involved. Sarah arranged this with our consent on the day and ensured it was approved appropriately by Dr Johnson (as part of the multidisciplinary medical team dealing with dad). The form would remain in a folder in the house should it ever be needed for reference.

We did talk a little about what might happen if/when dialysis stopped. She said she would run through the package of support available in detail should that time arise, but gave an indication of the additional support that would be provided and the implications for medication and general care.

I also asked about the process that would apply after dad passed away if that were to take place at home (rather than when out for dialysis) and she went through the steps in terms of calling the local GP in order for a death certificate to be issued; following up with the registrar and then allowing the undertaker's to remove the body. This would be a little different from what I had experienced with mum, as she had died in hospital (and in Leeds). That triggered a thought in my mind that I should ring up the undertaker's in Leeds and discuss the situation at some point sooner rather than later – as we would have the complication of an "out of town" death and needing to repatriate dad back to Leeds for the funeral.

At the end of all the discussions we paused for reflection. Andreas had been quiet throughout, listening to all the information and Sarah noticed this and asked him whether he had any comments/thoughts. He did say that he thought Ian would be better off in hospital and would receive better care there. Jacqueline immediately responded that she was not going to let him go into hospital and that she could provide better care (with support) at home. I agreed emphatically. I'm sure

Jacqueline and I were thinking the same thing – we had not come this far, over so many months of pain and suffering to give up now and pass over primary responsibility for dad in the final (and most important) period of his fading life.

Before she left Sarah did go up and spend some time talking to dad. One thing she did feedback was that she had asked him whether he would be okay staying at home if he couldn't get to dialysis for any reason – and he had nodded in reply. This was something we would end up revisiting in a few months' time.

The finality of what we were dealing with was re-emphasised just a couple of days later, when it was the anniversary of mum's passing ("*Yahrzeit*") – and as per the custom we lit a memorial candle (that would burn for twenty four hours) and said the prayer of mourning ("*Kaddish*"). It was difficult to believe that six years had gone by since that dark time.

That Tuesday brought a stark contrast in that it was the Queen's diamond jubilee celebrations, with it being declared a public holiday (after the normal bank holiday on the Monday). Like in thousands of places that day, our street in West End, Woking had a street party with all the associated celebrations. Linda and I wandered out of our house to socialise with everyone around lunch time, but then left to go to spend time with dad during the afternoon. The contrast of situations was extreme and very sad – lots of people out enjoying themselves and dad confined to bed just a short distance away, never to get out and take part in such events again. It was very sobering.

The following Monday (11th June) soon came around and brought the meeting with Dr Marsh, as well as the normal dialysis session. The arrangement was for Dr Marsh to see dad at the West Byfleet dialysis centre at 1 p.m. after which dad would proceed with his dialysis session as normal in the afternoon. This meeting was to prove probably the most upsetting and heart breaking we had experienced to date.

We arrived at the centre by ambulance transport as normal (Jacqueline generally used to go in the ambulance with dad and I followed behind in my car with all the myriad of things we brought along to make the session as comfortable as possible for him). On arriving at the centre Donna and Steve helped transfer dad into a wheelchair so we could use the lift to get up to the first floor of the building where the offices and consulting rooms were. Later when Dr Marsh found out we had done this he said he would have been happy to have left dad on the ambulance trolley and come down stairs to talk to him (that was the type of considerate and thoughtful person we had come to know over the years).

When we got to the consulting room Dr Marsh brought his chair around from behind the desk and we all sat in a circle. I was to dad's left and Jacqueline to his right, with Dr Marsh opposite dad to my left and the specialist nurse – Jackie – to Jacqueline's right. The session took around three quarters of an hour – for many reasons. We all realised what a critical meeting this was and the need to understand exactly dad's condition, his expectations and wishes and to run through all the various options available and implications. Also by this time (and given the added pain of sitting in a wheelchair again rather than lying on a bed) conversations with dad could be painfully slow. He was having great difficulty expressing himself at times and with his limited communication understanding "where he was at" was not always easy. At times his replies could be confused as well (for example he mentioned he was sometimes getting up at home, which had not actually been the case for quite a while).

Obviously, Dr Marsh had already gone through dad's medical notes, particularly with regards to his dialysis (including his regular blood test results, blood pressure on the dialysis sessions, amounts of fluid being taken off at each visit etc.). So the session was more around dad's overall state of mind and understanding/wishes. He said that he did like coming to dialysis in terms of seeing people and socialising – he mentioned Lyn (a younger lady on dialysis) and her daughter Chantelle with whom he had built up a good friendship through the visits (dad had even paid for them and Lyn's husband to come along to the pantomime at Woking with him and Jacqueline/Andreas on more than one occasion). He also mentioned the various staff members with whom he had built up close relationships. Dr Marsh did push him on more than one occasion as to whether he wished to continue coming to dialysis. Generally he said he wanted to continue, but later on he indicated it would be okay if he wasn't to come. He did say explicitly that he didn't want to die (!) and that he was concerned about certain things if he wasn't around (he specifically mentioned he was concerned that Jacqueline's marriage might break up – to which Jacqueline assured him that was solid and he shouldn't have any worries about that). This was typical of dad in that even in his darkest hour he was still thinking about other people. He said he had had a good life (interesting in that considering all the traumatic events he had endured over the years some people may not have been so positive looking back).

Then Dr Marsh asked the "killer" question. He asked dad what he saw happening in the near future. Dad thought for a moment and then quietly said "I'm hoping to get better". At this point Dr Marsh moved closer to dad (and I seem to remember took hold of his hands). He quietly and compassionately said to dad that unfortunately that was not going to happen; that he was a frail person and he was coming to the last stage in his life (which dad acknowledged). He then said that he wanted that stage to be as good as possible for dad and that the priority would be to relieve and manage his pain as much as possible and provide what quality of life he could whilst minimising the impact of the dialysis. He was quietly clear though that dad was going to die!!

Throughout this part of the session the emotional pain was intense for Jacqueline and I as well. We were both desperately trying to fight back the tears (not always successfully) as we were torn apart inside – not just by the actual prognosis, but by the obvious emotional as well as physical pain dad was going through by being told that he wasn't going to get better this time.

Again, Dr Marsh circled around to the question as to whether dad wished to cease dialysis in the circumstances. He carefully went through what the probable effects would be should that decision be taken (i.e. the likely scenario of how things would play out), but despite everything that had been said dad said he was not ready to make the decision to stop yet.

At the end of an emotionally exhausting and draining session Dr Marsh summarised where he thought we had got to – and his proposals. He said that the message from dad was not clear enough for *him* to take the decision to stop the dialysis sessions. However, in order to try and minimise the pain and stress on dad he proposed that the number of sessions be reduced from three to two per week (Monday and Friday). Although normally that would not be sufficient, he felt that if dad was spending all his time in bed and not consuming a lot of liquids, that two sessions would probably be just enough to clear most of the toxins building up in the bloodstream and take off what little fluid needed to come off, whilst obviating the need for the trauma that getting him to, through and back from a third session each week would create. He said he would arrange a three way session between Sarah Ivy, Jacqueline and I and himself to talk about pain management and adjust any medication accordingly. He also suggested that Jacqueline and I came back to see him briefly before clinic early the following morning to have a "wash up" after this session. On that note we left the room and took dad down stairs for his normal dialysis session.

Looking back I cannot have high enough praise for Dr Marsh at this session (and generally). He handled a painful and difficult situation in an extremely empathetic, kind, gentle yet clear way – fully taking into account dad's (and our) views and wishes. It is much easier for doctors to deal with straight forward diagnosis and treatment scenarios, but the situation he faced with dad needed the highest level of skills and understanding. In many ways that session was as difficult for him as it was for us. People are often very quick to criticise doctors, but rarely do they shower on them the praise they deserve. Also, the fact that he decided to let dad continue to dialyse at the West Byfleet centre was a brave and astute decision. A number of doctors would have taken the safer way out, saying that due to dad's extreme condition, heightened risks of major problems occurring on dialysis and the fact that satellite centres didn't have doctors on site he would now have to revert back to the main hospital (St Helier's) if he wished to continue with the dialysis. However, he realised that would run contrary to the aim of minimising the distress and pain for dad and so was prepared to run the risks of allowing him to continue at West Byfleet (with all the staff and friends he knew) – again a brave decision to be applauded in the circumstances.

When we got downstairs we communicated the essence of the session to the staff and particularly the reduction to two days a week – so they could change the arrangements (including transport) accordingly.

The following morning Jacqueline and I returned for 8:30 a.m. to see Dr Marsh on our own. He was quite open with us and indicated that he had gone into the session yesterday with the thinking that he would be stopping the dialysis given the circumstances, but that given dad's views and frame of mind he felt that would have been premature. He also felt that the balance of two days dialysis per week versus the standard three was probably the best solution at this point to minimise pain and discomfort for dad and given that his metabolism was now quite slow it would probably not prove to be too detrimental. We did seek advice as to how we should approach the situation, if/when it arose, that dad was not well enough to get to dialysis. Dr Marsh's view was that we should probably try one more time (for the next scheduled dialysis day) and if that also proved infeasible then to take that as the trigger to "leave it" at that point. Jacqueline and I were both obviously concerned about making such a decision, but Dr Marsh was quire re-assuring that it would normally be fairly clear when circumstances had got to the point where getting to and undertaking dialysis was no longer sensible or possible.

He did mention that obviously we may be faced with a situation at the centre where it was not possible to dialyse him for purely medical reasons – i.e. with his already low blood pressure, this may drop so low that dialysis was technically not possible. He said we should be cognisant of this possible outcome. In terms of how long we had left, this was difficult to quantify, but he felt it was likely to be weeks rather than months given his current condition. After thanking him again for his understanding and sensitive handling of the situation, we got up to leave with him saying to us that we should feel free to contact him or the specialist nurse, Jackie, at any time if needed.

We now had a level of clarity (which in many ways we wished we hadn't got) as to what we were facing and the relatively short timescales involved.

Chapter 8

One of the things we did during the rest of that week was to let close friends and relatives know what the situation was. Our cousin Leslie (in Leeds) said he would arrange to drop in to see dad soon as did Moira Gelman. They both were as good as their words over the next few weeks. Their visits always proved a positive fillip to dad – they proved a good stimulus and a change from just seeing Jacqueline and I all the time. We also advised our other cousin David, who said to let him know as things progressed!

I had been keeping my boss at work up to date with how things were progressing. I was now reporting into a Portfolio Director, Adam Cayley, having moved reporting lines a while ago when Yvonne Mowlds had gone on maternity leave. Adam was exceptional in terms of his caring and supportive approach – as Yvonne had been – and was very clear that I needed to do whatever was best in the circumstances; just to keep him and the rest of the team informed so they could cover/deal with work aspects as necessary. I was exceptionally fortunate to have had such outstanding managers during this traumatic time – it certainly helped to alleviate some of the pressure from the already intense situation. Every week before I left work I would produce a "status" email which set out exactly where we were with everything I was working on and any immediate follow up work required, should I suddenly not be able to come in to work for a while. They were fully aware that from the point of something happening it would be a couple of weeks before I could be back in the office (due to the funeral in Leeds and the week of mourning/prayers to be held there immediately following the funeral).

The Sunday following our session with Dr Marsh happened to be Father's Day and despite the situation we were all facing, Jacqueline and I were determined to make it as "normal" a Father's Day as possible. We got a Father's Day cake with candles spelling out the word "Dad", a lovely bouquet of flowers, balloons (including a large helium one) and cards. Although dad was eating and drinking very little, he did have a slice of the Father's Day cake with a little drink. In terms of drinks we had had to resort to using a plastic cup with a lid/spout on it, as trying to use a normal cup whilst lying in bed would have resulted in the drink being spilled all over. Although dad was looking particularly frail and gaunt at this time we did take a lot of pictures with him and us, the cake etc.

I can appreciate that when someone is that ill their family may feel awkward about taking photos on such occasions. It very much depends on the person's attitude. They may only wish to have photos remain after they are gone from when they were well – understandable. We had always taken lots of photos on such occasions in the past and so we continued to make the day as "normal" as we could and dad seemed quite relaxed about that. Looking back at the photos today I am glad we took them, albeit they bring back sweet and sour memories. In the end that time was a part of dad's life, just like the rest of his time with us.

Although we were certain the remaining time would be short we obviously had no idea as to the actual timescale events would run to. In reality we probably didn't expect to see July out with him still with us. Hence, there were various matters we needed to attend to sooner rather than later. One was to dad's spiritual needs. So far we had been concentrating on his physical condition rather than anything else as the primary concern. Now we knew that time was running out it was only right to try and ensure he had every support emotionally to see him through this period. Through contacts in Leeds Jacqueline obtained the details of a Rabbi from a synagogue not too far away (unfortunately there wasn't one locally). She arranged for him to come and spend some time with dad (with his agreement) as this might help bring a certain peace of mind and support his strong beliefs in the faith. The Rabbi came over around lunchtime one Wednesday towards the end of June. Although he tried to be as helpful and supportive as possible, his lack of experience in dealing with such circumstances meant that the visit was less than successful (in our eyes). Some weeks later we would try again, with a different, older and more experienced Rabbi, which would prove to be significantly more beneficial.

On a practical level Andreas installed another small TV in dad's bedroom. There had been one there for some time, but attached to a wall to the left of the bed. Now that dad's deterioration meant that generally he had to lie flat on his back all the time it was not possible to watch that TV. Hence, Andreas cabled through and suspended a TV from the ceiling in front of dad so he could watch it with ease. At least that provided some alleviation from the boredom of just lying in bed. We had also bought a portable radio/CD player which we had in the bedroom – as sometimes dad preferred to listen to music rather than having to try and concentrate on the TV. We also took the radio/CD player into dialysis as time went on (to be used with earphones) as it tended to have a calming effect on proceedings.

On a more sombre note there were two aspects I followed up on during June. One was to do with an enduring power of attorney and the other was the practicalities of future funeral arrangements. Although neither were pleasant, these were the sorts of practical matters that, if addressed now, would make matters that little less stressful as time went on.

In terms of the former, we had a power of attorney in place from way back in 2006 with Jacqueline and I being able to carry out dad's wishes on his behalf. This had allowed me to manage all his financial matters over the intervening years. However, this was predicated on the person being able to make decisions and we were simply the conduits through which he could implement them. Unfortunately, we were now at the stage where dad's ability to make decisions was obviously impaired. Under such circumstances it is necessary to apply to the Court of Protection – the Office of the Public Guardian – to have the power of attorney reviewed and registered in order that Jacqueline and I could then make independent decisions for dad in his best interests. The application form and requirements were quite extensive.

Apart from a lengthy application form (to accompany the existing power of attorney) there was also the need to write and send a form to all close relatives, informing them of the action being taken and allowing them a period of time to write to the Office of the Public Guardian and set out any objections they might have to this course of action (required by the Mental Capacity Act 2005). We talked to David and Leslie, who were the only living close relatives, to let them know what we were doing (and to expect the formal form). They had no objections in the circumstances, but we still had to let the required timescales pass before we could get confirmation of the registration of the power of attorney from the court. The advice to others is to start this process as soon as is feasible (and necessary) due to the paperwork and timescales involved. There is a fee as well for this registration, which amounted to £130 at the time we applied.

The other key matter to understand sooner rather than later was the practicalities of arranging the funeral back in Leeds and repatriating dad's body at the time. Obviously, we had the experience of what had happened with mum in 2006, but being out of town would change the process somewhat. A gentleman called Louis Burton (and his wife) had taken over the main burial business in Leeds since mum passed away. Our cousin Leslie knew him quite well and I gave Louis a call both to alert him to the situation and get his advice on what would need to be done (and by whom) when the time came.

He was extremely helpful and made it clear what he would do in Leeds, but even more importantly what we would be required to do in Surrey – a lot of which he would have arranged had we been local. We would have to arrange for a death certificate to be issued, to make an appointment at the Registry Office to record the death and attend accordingly. As we hoped that dad would be at home when the event happened we talked through the implications of that – in terms of whether we would need to find a local undertaker to remove and hold the body until he could come down to collect it (and whether the undertaker needed to be Jewish or not), or if we could keep the body at home until he arrived (and if so what practical steps would he advise during that time).

I also talked to a friend of mine in Leeds from boyhood times – Reverend Anthony Gilbert. He and I attended the Jewish evening classes up to the time I had my Jewish coming of age (*"Barmitzvah"*). He has since become a fully-fledged Rabbi. He was also extremely helpful in giving detailed practical advice on what we should and should not do if we decided to keep dad at home until Louis Burton could come down to collect him. Just in case things changed I subsequently contacted a local undertaker's and discussed the situation with them and obtained their 24 hour contact number, detail of fees etc., just in case we did need to avail ourselves of that temporary route. The final piece of the jigsaw was to determine which Registry Office would need to be used. That is not always as simple as you might think. In some areas there are satellite offices, so it is worth an early call to the main office to get them to advise who you should contact (given the anticipated place of death) and what the direct contact number is for appointments.

To some people all of this preparation may seem somewhat morbid or heartless, but I would challenge that. As I have reflected on before in this book, I believe that the more prepared you are for an event and the more you know what will need to be done (including various contact numbers) the better the chance of minimising the stress of the situation when it occurs. It is definitely one of the traits I inherited from dad (thinking ahead and trying to be prepared).

Over the next few weeks the dialysis sessions progressed twice a week as normal. They were always extremely stressful, with the distress dad suffered getting there and back. Also just getting him through the three and half hours was often an achievement in itself. Surprisingly in these early weeks his blood pressure was generally (just) managing to hold up – albeit it was very low compared with normal. However, the other challenge was the general pain his body was enduring – both from all the back deterioration and from his foot, where one toe was still quite black, plus the odd pressure sore that surfaced (despite every effort to avoid this). We often used the Oxynorm liquid before his dialysis and then again towards the end of the session to try and minimise the discomfort during the dialysis and for the journey home. Jacqueline and I would be there with him throughout the session (I was only working Tuesday and Thursday at that time), taking it in turns to sit with him and do everything necessary to minimise the pain/ get him through the session (including massaging his leg when it occasionally went into cramp and giving him a muscle relaxant if necessary). They seemed to be the longest three and a half hour periods we have ever experienced! Meanwhile, the angina episodes hadn't gone away and we were still dealing with those on a not infrequent basis.

Fortunately, we had built up a really close relationship with Graham, Donna and Steve (the ambulance team) and they went out of their way to help dad and make him as comfortable as possible. Graham even gave us his mobile number and said if we needed any help, at any time, just to ring him. They revealed to us that they used to be amused when they saw us taking everything but the kitchen sink into dialysis earlier that year to help dad be as comfortable as possible – but they now understood why we had been doing that and how beneficial it was in getting him through the dialysis sessions. Donna got on particularly well with dad and she seemed to have the ability to relieve some of his back pain from time to time. Sometimes he must have been laying in a position that was particularly causing pressure on a nerve and Donna had this technique of sliding both her hands under the lower part of his back and moving/straightening him slightly – which often reduced the pain. Jacqueline and I named it the "Donna manoeuvre" which she found amusing (we started to use it ourselves on occasions with dad).

The only scare I got from the team was one evening on our way back home from the centre. It was Friday night and the traffic was particularly heavy, so the journey was taking much longer than normal. I had set out just ahead of the ambulance, and just as we approached West End the blue lights of the ambulance flashed on behind me and the vehicle pulled out and made its way past (as the traffic pulled over/parted). My heart sank as I assumed there was a major problem with dad. I couldn't piggy back behind them on the road and started to get anxious that something would happen and I wouldn't be there with dad and Jacqueline. A few seconds later my hands free mobile rang in the car and it was Jacqueline. She said not to worry. Graham had got increasingly concerned at the length of the journey and the possible detrimental impact on dad, so he had made the decision to put on the blue lights so he could get him home and into bed quickly – panic over!

We did have a hiccup in the ambulance transfer arrangements for a short period. At one point the dialysis centre advised that the transfer operation would be carried out by a crew from the G4S transport organisation who did a lot of the other transport work for the NHS. We were sceptical, but willing to see how it went – not good! Although the two gentlemen were pleasant enough we had no confidence in the way they transferred dad. Taking him down the stairs in a chair seemed much more precarious with them than with the A2B crew and we had fears they were going to drop dad on more than one occasion. It only took two transfers for us to reach the decision to replace them. From previous experience we were prepared to re-engage A2B at our own cost (if necessary), but having discussed matters with the dialysis team we ended up having the A2B team re-instated to us to great relief all round.

In contrast to all the problems dad was enduring, the other medical problem that occurred involved me. It was a Friday evening early in July and we had just arrived home from dialysis with the ambulance. The crew had brought dad upstairs to the bedroom in the portable carrying chair and we were just getting ready to lift him into bed. I was in my usual place, crouched down with my hands under his bottom. We counted to three and lifted him up, but as I got up sharply and leant over the bed to put dad on it I had an excruciating pain down the back of my right thigh and we all heard something "pop". Just as dad touched the bed I hopped away in agony. It transpired that, having been sat down most of the afternoon, my hamstrings had stiffened up and by the explosive movement of standing up suddenly (with the weight of dad) I had torn some of the muscles around the right hamstring. Despite the pain it did provide some amusement to the crew with me hopping around on the landing!! They said they heard the "pop" as it tore.

It meant a visit to the GP early the following week and a bout of painkillers and cold and then warm compresses over time to improve the situation. For two or three weeks I had to walk around very slowly and carefully until the tear finally mended of its own accord – what do they say, timing is everything! That was the last thing I needed at that time, with all our efforts being focussed on looking after dad. To this day I still do stretching exercises most mornings and evenings to keep everything mobile and problem free.

Bart was still helping us out by spending an afternoon a week with dad and in fact put in a further (Saturday) afternoon in late July. Linda's brother and fiancée, Sue, were getting married on the weekend of the 21st/22nd July and obviously Linda and I wanted to be there. We would be back Sunday afternoon, so Bart kindly agreed to come and be with dad on the Saturday afternoon, when I would normally have been there.

The end of July saw the Olympic Games open in London. I must admit that I had not thought that dad would still be with us at this time, given how poor his condition was at the beginning of June. Other such thoughts permeated my mind from time to time – for example, it was now obvious that we had all spent our last Christmas together and that the end of this year would be very different. Considering I had always spent Christmas with mum and dad throughout my whole life it was a painful thought to realise that would never happen again. When such thoughts and emotions surfaced I tried to rise above them and just come back to concentrating on the present and what needed to be done.

August saw the gradual continuation of dad's deterioration, both physically and mentally. There were a number of angina episodes and often they were of a longer duration. He was using the oxygen generator much more frequently now – not just when he had an angina attack – and a nebuliser (to ensure that we kept his chest as clear as possible, given that he was lying down most of the time). His bedroom was becoming a little like a hospital room, with a special bed, electrically operated/inflated mattress, commode, turntable to get out of bed, oxygen tubes and the nebuliser etc., – but if that's what it took to keep him as comfortable as possible then so be it.

In addition to visits by the District Nurses we had been receiving some night time support from the specialist Beacon nurses. However, come late August Sarah Ivy informed us that, unfortunately, their last night would have to be the 24th August (at least for the time being). Although this was somewhat of a blow we could understand the logic. Those nurses were in short supply (and high demand) and they were normally only deployed when the patient had little time left. Back in June that seemed to be the situation with dad, yet here we were in late August still awaiting the inevitable.

Sarah did indicate that when the situation took a turn for the worse she would try and arrange the re-instatement of this support. Over the next few weeks we did avail ourselves of some night time support privately via Bluebird Care – a care agency based in Camberley.

It is interesting to pause for a moment and talk about various things we take for granted as a fit and able bodied person, but that could cause problems when bed bound. One example is going to the dentist. When we have a problem we make an appointment and go along to get it attended to. That was no longer possible with dad. Again, we were fortunate in having such an excellent and caring dentist. We all went to the same practice over in Weybridge. It comprised a husband and wife team – the Salters. At one point dad was having trouble with a tooth and initially we pursued the avenue of trying to get an appointment with a mobile dentist we had been advised of. However, this proved fruitless and would probably have taken weeks to arrange – which was really of no use to anyone. Jacqueline then rang and discussed the matter with Mrs Salters, who made the very generous offer of making a home visit (albeit that was not something they usually carried out).

Similarly dad used to have a chiropodist (Ellen Maxwell) visit every few weeks and despite his condition she agreed to visit over the summer to do what she could. Obviously, with his toe still being in a very bad condition and a pressure sore on his heel etc., she had to be very careful, but she did what she could in the circumstances. If you find yourself facing an extended period of caring for someone who is house or bed bound it is worth considering how you might avail yourself of such services if required and making contact with such people as soon as possible.

As time went on it became increasingly difficult for dad to get from the bed to the commode. It was always a struggle even with our help and support and a painful experience generally. Also, we had reached the stage where Jacqueline or I needed to help him "clean up" after sitting on the commode. In a hospital or care home there would have been a care assistant to do such things, but there was only Jacqueline and I to carry this out at home. It goes without saying that this was not the most pleasant of care duties to perform and I am sure many people would have found it impossible to do – but at the end of the day there was nobody else to do this, so you almost had to put yourself on automatic and get on with it. Obviously, we had latex gloves and cleansing foam to use, but it was still an unpleasant necessity. Mind you, the above gives my perspective, but the way dad was feeling must have been much worse. For someone who had spent his whole life looking after his family (having been such a strong figurehead) to be reduced to having his children having to do this for him must have been terrible. Jacqueline and I always passed this off if he mentioned it, saying it was no problem; not an issue; as we wanted to minimise his discomfort with the situation. After all he had enough to deal with!

The end of the first week in September provided us with the first taste of what was to become a more regular and extremely difficult scenario to deal with. Ian started to struggle even more with getting through the three and a half hour dialysis sessions. The first Friday in September saw him having to be taken off dialysis about forty minutes early, with problems generally in tolerating the stress of it and falling blood pressure. Such times were to prove a major strain and decision making challenge. We all new that with only attending dialysis twice a week he really needed to go through the full timespan. On the other hand, keeping him on dialysis if his blood pressure was dropping dangerously low and he was feeling in distress was not something we should be doing either – it proved to be a fine (and extremely difficult) balancing act.

We were in regular contact with Sarah Ivy at the hospice and kept her informed of the deteriorating situation and problems we were facing. Also, she was very good in providing advice in respect of changing conditions. For example, dad was starting to find it more and more difficult to swallow, which had a major implication in terms of the number of tablets he had been taking each day (for some years) for blood pressure, heart condition etc.

Late September found us facing the same sort of situation described above in terms of managing to get dad through the dialysis session. Both on the Monday and Friday of the week commencing 24th September he had to be taken off the dialysis machine around half an hour early due to a combination of problems (including dangerously low blood pressure). When we say low we are talking about 60's over 40's (systolic to diastolic pressure) where a normal persons' pressure may be around 120 over 80!! If this situation continued we knew we would be reaching the point Dr Marsh referred, to back in June, where the dialysis sessions would not be feasible any more.

The Saturday evening of that week saw us receiving a visit from Rabbi Dubov. After the previous visit we had been exploring the possibility of someone else visiting dad through our cousin and contacts in Leeds. The recommendation of Rabbi Dubov proved to be ideal. He spent a considerable amount of time with dad that evening and then time with Jacqueline and I, downstairs, talking about things from our perspective and giving advice/answering our questions.

The time he spent with dad was an emotionally painful one for all of us. We generally let the two of them have time alone, but were also popping in and out of the bedroom from time to time to "help along" the conversation as best we could. This was because dad's ability to communicate was quite poor at this stage and also the clarity of things he was telling Rabbi Dubov was not always there. They talked a bit about dad's life and what he had done, although sometimes he seemed to get stuck in a "loop" going over the same topic a number of times. One of the things dad really tried to impress on Rabbi Dubov was that he had tried to be a good man all his life and could never remember hurting anyone (in fact he was always trying to help other people).

After a while the Rabbi suggested that the two of them said some prayers together, so we got dad his prayer book and put his yarmulke (skull cap) and glasses on. The main prayer that was read was the "*Shema*". This was the same prayer that dad had read at mum's bedside when she was dying in Leeds! Unfortunately, dad had deteriorated so much that he had great difficulty saying the prayer (in Hebrew) whereas in years gone by he would have known it virtually off by heart. Rabbi Dubov was very sensitive to this and suggested they say it one word at a time with him first and then dad repeating each word afterwards – which they managed to do.

After his time with dad he spent further time with Jacqueline and I in the living room, as he felt it was just as important that we had the help and support we needed as well as dad. We took the opportunity to run over the possible scenarios that might occur when the time came and got his advice and guidance on what to do and what not to do – generally it was consistent with the information I had obtained from my conversations with people in Leeds, but it was always good to get confirmation and re-iteration of that.

The difficulty in getting dad through the dialysis sessions continued and grew in October. We were finding that the amount of fluid they set the machine up with (to take off) at the start of the session was often having to be reduced part way through as the blood pressure dropped and the strain on the body increased. This was now becoming a regular challenge we faced each time.

On a brighter note, in the midst of all this gloom, dad amazingly reached his ninety fifth birthday on the 16th October. None of us could have possibly imagined back in June that we would have the opportunity to celebrate this last birthday. His actual birthday was on the Tuesday, but we had an "open house" on the previous Sunday afternoon so that any friends or family could visit. Jacqueline set up a great spread of food (as always) in the conservatory and people tended to come for a period of time, go up and see/talk to dad in bed and also socialise and grab a bite to eat downstairs. We had to stagger the time people spent with Ian as at this stage he tired very quickly. We had a speciality birthday cake made comprising some teddy bears sitting around a white tablecloth having a picnic on a green lawn, with icing replicas of various food and "*Happy 95th Birthday Dad*" written across the bottom of the cake. There was also the full gamut of balloons, flowers and birthday cards in dad's room with him.

It was heart-warming to see how many people dropped in during the day – Moira Gelman was down from Leeds; Bart and his wife Aga and their young baby came by; the next door neighbours Martin and Rob spent time with Ian, as well as some of Jacqueline's friends (Carol and Rowena) and even Puspa (who came and did housework/cleaning for Jacqueline each week). There were many others, but I will spare you the cast list at this time. In some ways it was an unusual feeling in that everyone knew this would be the last birthday for dad and for most of them the last time they would see him alive. I suppose looking back it could be taken more as a celebration of his life, not just the fact that it was another birthday. We took plenty of photos of him with each of the people who dropped in and despite the impending situation he was smiling with them and trying to communicate as best he could at that time. He did manage to blow out the candles on the cake and have a small piece with a drink. It was all a brief respite from the day to day trauma we were all going through.

As the clocks went back at the end of October, so the hour glass of dad's life was gradually running out. The following week proved to be pivotal in determining the final amount of time left. By this time I always dreaded the phone ringing at home, especially from late evening onwards, as it only meant one thing – a call from Jacqueline to let me know there was some sort of immediate problem. Unfortunately, it had happened on a number of occasions over recent months and every time the phone rang my heart would sink and my stomach start to knot up – what issue were we facing this time? Invariably it would mean getting out of bed, getting dressed and going up the road to help Jacqueline deal with whatever was facing us. In the early hours of Thursday morning (1st November) I got another of these calls. Dad was having sever angina pains and even the GTN spray and oxygen did not seem to be alleviating the situation. It was about two a.m. and I jumped out of bed to get ready and dash up the road – only about five minutes' drive away at that time of the morning.

I had a black cloth carrier bag I bought on a holiday in Bermuda and for some time now had kept a lot of items in there that I might need in such circumstances – ready to be picked up and taken in an emergency. I took it with me whenever I was out of the house. It had all the medical paperwork re dad's dialysis, a medication list, a copy of the "do not resuscitate" form, all the contacts I might need such as the undertaker, registry office, friends and relatives etc., and various personal items like a shaver and contact lens case (for my lenses). I picked this up and headed for Laird Court.

The next couple of hours were difficult in the extreme. Despite the use of the GTN spray and putting dad on oxygen he was still having severe chest pains. Over the next hour Jacqueline and I tried everything, including muscle relaxants and pain relief to try and alleviate the pain. At one point dad did say to call an ambulance, despite the fact that in the past he had always tried to dissuade us from such action in similar circumstances. It was a critical dilemma for Jacqueline and I. We knew that calling for an ambulance would only cause more pain and distress for dad initially (trying to move him to get him into the ambulance and to hospital), plus even if that took place there would be hours of discomfort in Accident & Emergency, most likely to be followed by admission to a ward. If that happened the likelihood of getting him home again was minimal, given his weak condition, and so we could end up having gone through everything that year for him to end up dying in hospital after all!!

We kept trying to do what we could and at one time the thought flashed through my mind, as I am sure it did for Jacqueline, that we could actually be witnessing the end. We held our nerve and eventually the pain started to gradually subside – it appeared we had made the correct call. I would say that was probably the most difficult decision we had ever made in our lives. It was a terrible feeling potentially having someone's life in your hands and being forced into making such a decision (made doubly worse by it being close family). Eventually, I made my way back home around six o'clock in the morning – just as Linda was getting up for work.

To use that quote again from the Jaws movie *"just when you thought it was safe to go back in the water…"* unfortunately, the end of that week threw up another just as intense a situation and decision on dialysis.

That Friday afternoon proved to be a very difficult dialysis session right from the start. It took a while to get dad's blood pressure up to a passable level to start the dialysis and once started, the session was a massive struggle for him throughout. He seemed to be in discomfort from the word go. We did everything we could think of to help and make him as comfortable as possible and at one point the staff decided not to take any further fluid off in order to minimise his distress; but despite everything we only got about two hours into the three and a half hour session when we hit a major problem. Dad's blood pressure continued to drop to a dangerously low level and he started to say to us to take him off (that he couldn't stand it any longer). Sometimes in the past we had the odd occasion when he wanted to come off – usually much nearer to the end of the session – and we had managed to get him through the remaining time, but this time was different. He became more and more agitated and distressed. The staff were there with us round the bed assessing the situation and eventually Iris (his "named" nurse) advised that he needed to come off the dialysis machine. Jacqueline and I instantly realised that should that happen it was unlikely he would dialyse again! Having to make that sort of decision, knowing it potentially could set the clock ticking on the final days of a person's life, is an awful position in which to be placed.

I looked at dad suffering on the bed, desperate to be alleviated from his distress and cognisant that if the blood pressure dropped any lower he may well die there and then in the dialysis centre. From somewhere deep inside I dragged up the last shreds of my objectivity and realised there was only one compassionate and sensible decision – to take him off. I said this to Jacqueline who, naturally reacted very emotionally and didn't want to do that – there were some barbed words aimed at me, which I realised were more due to the extreme emotions and pain she was experiencing than anything else. I reminded her that Dr Marsh said we should all be aiming to make dad's time left as comfortable as possible and to minimise any distress – by trying to keep him on the dialysis we would be going against that ethos.

After a couple of minutes (that seemed like an eternity), Jacqueline finally agreed and we said to Iris to take him off the machine – we had only made it through two hours and five minutes of the session. It was appropriate, in some way, that it was Iris who was on duty that afternoon and that it was her who took dad off for what was to prove the last time, as she was the nurse who had put dad on to dialysis at his first session at the West Byfleet centre back in the summer of 2007. Those five years seemed to have gone by so quickly.

Once dad became stable and more settled we got in contact with the ambulance crew to see if they could return a bit earlier to take us home. We also discussed the ongoing situation with the staff at the centre. Iris questioned whether we wanted to cancel the forthcoming session on Monday (along with the transport). At that point we said "no" but said we would be in touch if there was any subsequent change in that decision. Jacqueline and I knew that there was a critical decision to be made over the coming weekend (in conjunction with dad, as far as possible) in terms of whether we had come to the end of the road as far as the dialysis was concerned, or whether we should try again on Monday.

We didn't discuss the matter any further that evening after getting dad home and to bed, but we did start to consider the situation on Saturday when I came round. I remember Jacqueline and I stood in the kitchen talking through what was the best/right option. The more I had thought about it during the previous evening the more I was convinced that we had reached the tipping point. The whole aim of reducing dad's dialysis sessions to two per week plus getting all the help/support that was necessary (including medication) was to minimise his pain and discomfort during whatever time he had left. Forcing him to continue to dialyse and endure the pain and suffering we saw on Friday afternoon ran contrary to what we were trying to achieve in my mind. My emotional side wanted to run full tilt away from that decision and its inevitable consequences, yet my objective side new it was the right decision – for dad. Jacqueline understood all the elements of the argument on both sides, but was quite honest on that Saturday in that she had not quite reached the point I had at that time and needed to think it through and discuss it further – totally understandable. It was like an athletics race – all the participants don't reach the finish line at the same time, but they do all have the same overall goal in mind.

When we talked again on Sunday Jacqueline said that she had now reached the same place that I had. However, the key element would be to try and explain the options to dad and get some sort of response/preference from him (if possible) on Monday morning, before the transport was due to arrive.

The Monday morning proved to be another extremely difficult time for us all. Jacqueline and I sat down with dad and tried to set out the two options we were all faced with, as simply as possible. These were either (a) to go to dialysis and try to continue with it – which had the risk that, similar to Friday's session, it may go wrong and there was a possibility we might not be able to bring him home (he could pass away at the centre), or (b) he could remain at home, in bed, but that would mean he would not be able to go to dialysis again and he would only have a further week or two with us.

It was difficult to decide whether he fully understood what we were explaining to him, though we repeated it a number of times and in as simple a manner as possible over quite a long time period. Because he found great difficulty speaking now, we indicated that all he needed to say was either "dialysis" or "home" and we would understand. It probably took the best part of an hour to get to an answer, but eventually dad mouthed "home"; "stay home". To be sure, we went over this more than once to try and ensure we had received the right message. During this time one of the district nursing staff arrived (as normal) and understanding the gravity of the situation, she also tried to help us so that dad understood and that we were confident we had received the message he wanted to convey. Having determined what was happening we rang the dialysis centre to advise them of the decision. The transport was already on its way, so we said we would explain to them when they arrived.

In hindsight, I can only imagine what feelings dad must have been experiencing when faced with the two options above. I know how painful it was for Jacqueline and I to reach, what we believed, was the best decision in the circumstances, but effectively we were asking someone – do you want to die in a week or two's time, or do you want to take a high risk of dying at a dialysis centre/not being at home when you pass away? What a horrendous decision for anyone to have to make!!

Just when we thought the roller coaster had finally stopped it gave a final twist. When the ambulance crew arrived I went outside to explain to them what had happened and the decision not to dialyse any more (to save them getting the equipment out of the ambulance). I was somewhat surprised to find three of them there instead of the usual two. As well as Donna and Steve, as normal, Graham (the boss) had come along as well. I realised afterwards that after Friday's episode he had probably been quite astute realising that the Monday morning could be a difficult time, no matter what decision we had come to, and had decided to come along to help and support us as well.

I expected them to disappear as they wouldn't now be needed, but that was not the case. Graham said they would come in and stay with us for a while (much appreciated). We made them a hot drink and we discussed things with them. We asked if any of them would like to go up to see dad (as it would be the last time they would have the opportunity). Steve said thanks, but declined, and decided to sit cross legged on the kitchen floor with his cuppa! Graham explained to me that Steve didn't handle such situations that well and would find it too upsetting going up to see dad in the circumstances. It showed how fond and attached they had become of him over the previous few months. Donna said she would like to and went up to talk to him.

However, after a few minutes she came back down stairs and said that dad was getting very agitated, indicating that Jacqueline and I were not doing what he wanted to do! Our heart sank; had we completely misinterpreted him and he *did* wish to continue with the dialysis? We went upstairs and talked to him again. After a while we suddenly realised what the problem was. He had seen Donna in her uniform and assumed that they were going to take him to dialysis as normal – exactly what he did NOT want. We explained that was not the case, that he was staying at home as he wanted and that Donna had just come up to see him, not take him to the centre. Crisis over!

The crew stayed with us for some time, to give us moral support, and Graham was quite honest with us at one point, as he could see we were still wrestling with whether the right decision had been taken. He said that looking at dad's condition and everything that had happened recently, he would have taken the decision NOT to take dad to dialysis that morning if we had not made it. He would have indicated that Ian was not fit to travel. It gave us a crumb of comfort that a more independent professional would have arrived at the same conclusion.

During that day we also contacted Sarah Ivy to let her know about the change in situation and discuss the next week or two. We went through the approach to medication (the Fentanyl patches and the Amitriptylene) as well as dad's breathing difficulties (she indicated they could give him an injection which might help with that). She said she would chat to the district nurse (Margaret) regarding the change in circumstances/best way forward and also would get back in touch with the Beacon nurses to try and re-instate some night cover (probably around three nights a week). As it turned out they managed to provide a night nurse *every* night for the remainder of dad's time. Sarah came in to see us on the Wednesday afternoon to see how we all were and talk further about what we should/could expect over the coming days.

Obviously, at the dialysis centre Bart was aware that Ian hadn't come in for his session. Jacqueline gave him a ring later to bring him up to speed with everything. He was due to spend the Tuesday afternoon with dad, but we indicated that wasn't necessary in the circumstances. However, he said he would like to come one last time; with which we were comfortable.

He spent the afternoon upstairs with dad and both Jacqueline and I were downstairs when he came down to leave. He gave each of us a hug and turned to go – then stopped. We could see that he had started to cry! He had grown very fond of dad over the years and I think it suddenly hit him that he wouldn't ever see him again. We sat him down and got him a cup of tea (a typically English thing to do). He kept apologising, understanding what Jacqueline and I must be going through, but we said it was fine. We were warmed to see somebody else who cared for dad enough that his imminent loss had moved them to tears.

The district nurses were now coming in a couple of times each day to help and do whatever they could for dad. He was now so weak that he wasn't even managing to get out of bed to use the commode. Consequently the nurses supplied special sheeting etc., and helped clean/change everything when they came in. Even this proved quite traumatic for dad at this stage. We used to help the nurses gently roll dad alternately onto one side and then the other so they could deal with matters and change the sheeting. There was even a technique to this as we learned from the nurses. They would use a spare pillow to put behind Ian's back and hold onto that so it was softer than holding onto dad himself. However, even doing this (and as quickly as possible) he was in extreme pain each time and often pleaded for us to stop – unfortunately it was a necessary evil; something we just had to do. Obviously his body was so weak that any movement generated unbearable pain!

I was due to work Wednesday and Thursday that week, but with Sarah Ivy coming round on Wednesday I took that off as leave. I rang my boss (Adam Cayley) and set out what had happened and the timescales we were now faced with. My intention was to come in on

Thursday and make that my last work day for a couple of weeks or so (depending upon how things played out). As always Adam was one hundred percent supportive and indicated I should take off as much leave as I wanted – we would sort out the admin once I got back. He was quite relaxed if I didn't want to come in on the Thursday, but I wanted to tie up some loose ends and ensure everything was in a state for other people to deal with for as long as I was off.

We talked to relatives and friends during the first couple of days of that week to let them know how circumstances had changed and the short timescale we were now facing. I also had another word with the undertaker to alert him to the circumstances, given the additional challenge of the repatriation to Leeds.

As we moved into the week commencing 12th November dad was becoming even weaker as we had been led to understand. Unfortunately he had also developed thrush inside his mouth and throat and we were using a spray on this to try and minimise the discomfort therefrom. Generally he was in a calm state although there were instances where he became more agitated. Thankfully, the nurses only had to utilise the stock of injection vials in the house on the odd occasion to keep things as calm as possible and minimise the pain.

It was a strange period emotionally as you can imagine. There was no longer any lack of clarity over what was going to happen and the timescales were now clear as being days rather than weeks or months.

Both Jacqueline and I spent a lot of time sitting with dad in these last days, occasionally talking – albeit his communication now was virtually non-existent. The piece of advice I would give to anyone in a similar situation is not to wait too long to have any important, heart-to-heart conversations with someone in a deteriorating condition, as fate may suddenly rob you of this time and capability. We would put on the TV or a calming music CD in his bedroom, but generally it elicited little response. Sometimes I would ask dad whether he wanted the TV left on or some music put on instead, but often he would just continue staring at the TV screen and not respond – an emotionally painful and frustrating situation for me (seeing him having deteriorated to this extent). Sometimes we did put on some gentle background music on the portable CD player, which hopefully proved soothing. Each evening I would give dad a kiss, tell him I loved him and return home wondering whether the phone would ring, before the next time I was due up at Jacqueline's, with the dreaded call.

Chapter 9

The days slowly ticked by and dawn broke on Friday 16th November. Amazingly this was a full two weeks since we had to take dad off dialysis (early) for the last time. As with everything in Ian's life he had fought to the very last, as Dr Marsh had indicated the maximum time he anticipated dad lasting after stopping dialysis was one to two weeks.

I don't know whether in all his extensive reading dad had ever read any of Dylan Thomas's work, but his *"Do not go gentle into that good night"* poem to me had summed up dad's resilience and attitude throughout his later years. It goes as follow:

"Do not go gentle into that good night,
Old age should burn and rave at close of day,
Rage, rage against the dying of the light.

Though wise men at their end know dark is right,
Because their words had forked no lightning they
Do not go gentle into that good night.

Good men, the last wave by, crying how bright,
Their frail deeds might have danced in a green bay,
Rage, rage against the dying of the light.

Wild men who caught and sang the sun in flight,
And learn, too late, they grieve it on its way,
Do not go gentle into that good night.

Grave men, near death, who see with blinding sight,
Blind eyes could blaze like meteors and be gay,
Rage, rage against the dying of the light.

And you, my father, there on the sad height,
Curse, bless me now with your fierce tears, I pray.
Do not go gentle into that good night.
Rage, rage against the dying of the light."

The time was between seven and eight o'clock in the morning. Linda had already left for work and I had just finished getting dressed when the phone rang. It was Andreas rather than Jacqueline, who I had expected. All he said was that Jacqueline had asked him to ring and had said that I should come round straight away – I said I was on my way. I grabbed all my bits and pieces as normal and set off for Laird Court. It was only a few minutes' drive away, but it seemed to take an eternity at that time. I was stealing myself for what was to come (as best I could). I parked up opposite the house and as I walked over Andreas opened the door and let me in. As I stood in the hallway Jacqueline was coming down stairs. I looked up at her face and my heart sank – even before she said a word I knew what had happened. As she reached the bottom of the stairs all she said was "he's gone"! We just held each other and cried.

No matter how many years you spend trying to prepare yourself for that moment and how much certainty you have as to when it is coming the feeling when it happens is devastating and overwhelming. The realisation that the two people that had given life to you and been there for you throughout all your days were no longer on this earth is more than you can come to terms with in that instant.

After a minute Jacqueline asked if I wanted to go upstairs and I said yes. It is interesting that as I walked into the bedroom and looked at dad's dead body for the first time I didn't have the awful reaction I had experienced with mum in hospital. Whether it was the "benefit" of having had such an experience once; the fact that with dad we had been expecting this for some time; or the comfort of knowing that he was finally out of his pain and distress I really don't know. I leant over, kissed him on the forehead and said something like "*goodbye dad, I love you*". Finally, all the fighting was over (for all of us) and he was at peace.

Jacqueline said that she had been sat with him and he had suddenly opened his eyes and looked around becoming more animated than he had been for some time. She had asked Andreas to call the district nurse as he might need an injection etc. When he got through Andreas seemed to be having difficulty explaining the situation so Jacqueline stepped out of the bedroom to take over the call and talk to the nurse. When she stepped back into the room shortly afterwards she suddenly realised dad seemed to have stopped breathing – him opening his eyes was to take a last look at this world and then he had quietly slipped away.

After a constant backdrop of urgency that had pervaded looking after dad for so long all of a sudden there was a calmness and no rush. We knew we needed to call the GP surgery initially, to arrange for a doctor to come out and certify the death, but we just sat in the room for a few minutes letting the enormity of what had happened sink in. Eventually Jacqueline rang the surgery and explained the situation. Although the doctors were already seeing patients at the surgery that morning they made arrangements for one of the lady doctor's to come out as soon as possible. My first call was to Linda to let her know what had happened (she would need to take some time off work at short notice to go up to Leeds with us all). It's funny, but although generally I was relatively calm in myself, once I started to try and talk about what had happened to Linda the emotions overwhelmed me and I had difficulty getting out what I wanted to say coherently. She said she would come home straight away, to which I indicated there was no need, as we were going to have to spend the next few hours sorting out matters. However, she was determined to be there to give me any further support I needed and when I dropped back home a little while later she was just arriving back from work as well.

The next call I made was to the Registry Office in Guildford to obtain an appointment to register the death and obtain all the required paperwork. They had one slot at 10:40 a.m. later that morning, if I could make that with the required paperwork. As the GP had agreed to come out so quickly I indicated I should be able to make that time. The GP arrived, carried out her examination and indicated she would go back and type up the death certificate for dad. Due to the tight timescale with the Registry Office I offered to come back with her, wait in the surgery and pick up the paperwork as soon as she had finished it. One thing that has always stuck in my memory was a comment from one of the receptionists at the surgery. Obviously, some of the other patients had to wait a bit longer as a result of the doctor dealing with the paperwork and as the receptionist handed the death certificate to me in an envelope, she said that I had been very "lucky" to get the doctor to do this at such short notice. I was in no mood for a fight that day, so I just glowered at her. I felt like saying "yes, I'm very lucky that my father has just died!!" I really would have expected more sensitivity from someone in that position.

Jacqueline had been making some phone calls to the family and friends while I was out. When I got back I said I was going to drop back home for some items, call the undertaker in Leeds and then make my way over to Guildford to register the death. Just as I got home (and met Linda on her way in) the phone rang. It was Louis Burton, the undertaker from Leeds, ringing me! He had been called by my cousin in Leeds to let him know what had happened and he decided to be pro-active in ringing me to make appropriate arrangements. Unfortunately, with the Jewish Sabbath starting around tea time on the Friday there was not enough time for him to come down, pick dad's body up and get it back to Leeds in time. He did say that instead of leaving it until Sunday he would be prepared to set off for London on Saturday evening (after the Sabbath had ended) albeit they probably wouldn't reach us until around 11 p.m. He would then take the body straight back to Leeds and try and arrange the funeral for the Sunday afternoon (something he would follow up and confirm later). I indicated that would be appreciated and that I would let Jacqueline know when I got back to her.

Having grabbed some additional paperwork Linda and I set off for the Registry Office in Guildford for the 10:40 appointment. It was quite ironic, but when we finally got in to see the Registrar it transpired it was a lady called Rosie Cooper – the same person who had officiated at Linda and my wedding a few years earlier (and she recognised us)! She expressed her condolences in the circumstances and proceeded to register the death and complete all the paperwork accordingly. Things seemed to have moved on and become more efficient since I had registered mum's death back in 2006. Whereas in the past I had to advise all interested parties separately about the death, this time the Registrar (via their system) would automatically advise various government departments regarding Ian's state pension, teacher's pension, driving licence and Blue Badge for parking etc. She actually took the Blue badge from me at the time (which I had brought along with all the paperwork). As with mum I asked for additional copies of the death certificate, which were swiftly printed off, and after about twenty minutes in total we were on our way back home. A person spends a lifetime in this world and yet about twenty minutes administration ties up their leaving it!

Linda and I made our way back to Laird Court to catch up with Jacqueline and let her know what Louis Burton had said and the timetable to which we would be working. She had been busy calling the Synagogue in Leeds, and further friends and family to let them all know of the situation. Although we had researched the option of using a local undertaker temporarily until Louis could arrive, Jacqueline and I discussed it further and she indicated she wanted to keep dad at home for the short period of time (less than a couple of days) – I concurred. Andreas did query this given that we had originally anticipated using a local undertaker as a stop gap, but Jacqueline was adamant that she wanted dad's body to remain at home.

We also talked to Moira and David Gelman to double check that their offer for us to hold the prayers of mourning (sitting *"Shiva"*) for the week after the funeral at their home in Leeds still stood. Despite the fact that we had similar offers from our cousins, holding the prayers at Moira and David's felt right – you could see mum and dad's old flat across the road from their house and Moira had remained in very close contact with dad even after he left Leeds (visiting on many occasions and telephoning every week). Despite the fact they were actually planning to move house within the next few weeks they said they would be honoured to do it.

During that Friday one of the Beacon nurses, who was due to come around, rang to ask whether it would still be okay for her to drop in given the circumstances, as she would like to see dad for one last time – we said of course. She spent time with Jacqueline and I when she came and then went up to see dad. I happened to be on the upstairs landing when she was in the bedroom with dad and remember the simple, but lovely, words she said. She hoped he was now at peace and said "have a safe journey, Ian"

We had a call back from Louis Burton during the day confirming that with him coming down late on the Saturday night, he had been able to arrange the funeral for 2 p.m. on the Sunday afternoon (18th November). That allowed us to get back in touch with friends and family and let everyone know the exact time and place (should they be able to make it). Knowing the exact timescale also meant we could arrange hotel accommodation in Leeds. We booked the Holiday Inn at Garforth, near Leeds, as it had become the "default" hotel we had used when visiting Leeds in recent years.

Over the next day or so Jacqueline and I spent various periods of time sitting with dad in the bedroom.

We had double checked that the religious requirement not to leave the body unattended didn't mean that someone had to be actually in the bedroom at all times, as long as there was someone in the house and no "stranger" could gain access. Jacqueline spent some of the time reading from a prayer book whilst I spent the time more generally in contemplation. The relatively short period of time also allowed us to pack and prepare generally for the time we would spend in Leeds. I emailed work to let them know what had happened and when I finally expected to be back in the office.

Saturday night came around fairly quickly. I had mixed feelings. In one respect I was quite pleased, as there had already started to be changes in dad's body – his eyes were becoming more sunk in his head etc. However, once Louis took the body away it would be the last time I would ever see dad or be able to touch him.

There was a delay in Louis and his wife arriving due to an unfortunate mistake. He rang us to say that he had gone to fill up the van before setting off and had used the wrong fuel!! Fortunately he realised this before driving off, but this obviously delayed his journey whilst the AA came out to syphon out the wrong fuel etc. I seem to remember it was getting on for 11 p.m. when they finally arrived. We had a cup of tea first and then Louis, Jacqueline and I went upstairs. He had brought in a hammock/cradle type item. It was made of material, with a number of longitudinal poles sewn into it. We would need to move dad's body onto this before it could be wrapped up and carried downstairs to a trolley, which we would then use to move it into the back of the van.

This proved to be a more upsetting event than I had imagined. Given dad's position in bed we had to actually lay out the item on the floor by the bed and then move and lift his body out of bed and on to the wrapping. It took all three of us to do this and was complicated by the fact that certain bodily fluids had solidified over the last couple of days. We eventually managed it and Louis continued wrapping up the body, securing it with ties accordingly. In order to bring the body down the narrow stairs it was only really feasible for two people to carry it (at the head and toe ends) and I said to Jacqueline that I would do that (she often had troubles with her lower back and now was not the time to put it out/have a major problem)!

Slowly Louis and I made our way out of the bedroom and down the stairs. I was actually surprised at how heavy the body was – considering dad was only about five foot three inches tall and had obviously lost a lot of weight over the previous months. We finally reached the bottom of the steps and lifted the body onto the trolley set up there. We then moved the trolley out of the front door, down the pathway and into the back of the van (where you could collapse the trolley legs so everything was flat on the floor of the van). Again, as I looked at this scene I found it profoundly upsetting and undignified. No matter what we've done or achieved in our lives and how good we have been is this what we are all reduced to – a cold body on the floor of an empty van? Despite the late hour the next door neighbours – Martin and Rob – came out to pay their last respects to dad before Louis and his wife drove off into the night. There was no rest for the four of us left though, as Linda and I set off shortly afterwards to drive up to Leeds with

Jacqueline and Andreas close behind – we actually arrived at the Holiday Inn around three in the morning!

The Sunday brought back déjà vu thoughts from 2006 and mum's funeral. We made our way over to Moira's house after lunch, where the official car was to pick us up. It took us down to the Beth Hamidrash Hagadol Synagogue on Street Lane, just a few minutes away, where we met up with the hearse. Again some of the family and friends were also there with their cars (other people would go directly to the cemetery on Gelderd Road). Considering what we had been through with dad's body over the last couple of days I was surprised that the sight of the coffin in the hearse had a dramatic effect on me again as I got out of the car at the synagogue. I dissolved into uncontrollable tears and sobbing, needing to turn and walk away from the hearse until I could regain some control. The various customs (which I have described earlier in this book) took place at the synagogue and then we all set off for the cemetery.

As I got out of the car at the cemetery I immediately saw my close friends Hazel and Jim Wilton walking towards me. I just put my arms around Hazel and we hugged – she looked absolutely devastated and was in an awful state. Hazel and Jim had always been close to mum and dad, often visiting them in Leeds even when Linda and I weren't there. Also Hazel had experienced losses in her family akin to ours so there was a special affinity in this situation. I shook Jim's hand and said thanks for coming, then turned to go into the cemetery.

The service followed the same course as mums' with the initial part being conducted in the small building at the entrance to the cemetery, before the coffin and congregation moved slowly to the graveside. I had provided those officiating with some summary details which they would use when talking about dad's life and they asked whether anyone else would like to say anything – at which Moira stepped up and communicated some heartfelt thoughts. It was gratifying to see that there were senior representatives from *three* of the synagogues in Leeds (not just the one we were currently a member of) which along with masonic colleagues indicated the esteem in which dad was held by the community. Moving down to the graveside had a different feel to last time. There was no-one else to look after this time – no dad to push down in his wheelchair and take care of. It was just a lonely walk for Jacqueline and I with our other halves.

The graveside was different as well. There was a cloth draped over the double headstone (to which dad's details would be added the following year) and the surrounds had been removed to allow the hole to be dug next to mums' grave accordingly. The remainder of the service took place, including Jacqueline and I reciting the prayer of mourning ("*Kaddish*") and dad's coffin was slowly lowered into the ground. As before we each took turns in shovelling earth into the grave to cover the coffin and finally the service was concluded. People started to leave the graveside and cemetery and eventually after some reflective time we made our move as well. Walking slowly away from the grave was the loneliest feeling I can remember – leaving dad (and mum) behind forever. It would be a very difficult world to come to terms with (and live in) from now on.

I don't remember much (if any) conversation going back to Moira's in the car. She had prepared some traditional food for us post the funeral which was much appreciated. We also lit a special candle that would burn for seven days, whilst we had the week of prayers. The first of the evening prayer sessions took place that evening (around 7 p.m.). Each evening's prayers were conducted by a different person, not only from our current synagogue but from other one's in Leeds as well. Again, it emphasised the high regard for dad in the Jewish community in Leeds. It was warming to hear most of them talk about dad and their fond memories of him at the end of each of the evening sessions – it made you realise that it wasn't just the family memories that lingered on, but those in the people he met and touched over his lifetime.

At the beginning of the week we made a visit to the offices of the Jewish Telegraph paper in Leeds to arrange a notification to be placed in the "Deaths" column for the next couple of weeks. It read as follows:

HARRIS
Ian

Passed away on Friday, November 16, aged 95.

Devoted husband of the late Fay.
Adored father of Jacqueline and Russell.
Loved and respected father-in-law of Andreas and Linda.
Forever in our thoughts and hearts.

May his dear soul rest in peace.

Linda returned to Surrey by train later on the Tuesday of that week and Andreas then decided to drive back on the Wednesday, as both had to return to work. I was quite relaxed about this as it gave Jacqueline and I a few days with only the two of us together to ponder on what had happened and the future.

Usually we would spend time during the day visiting friends and relatives, or doing some bits of shopping (it was coming up to the festival of lights ("*Hanukkah*") in December so we needed to buy some greeting cards and candles for that time). We would then go over to Moira and David's house around tea time and stay for the rest of the evening. They had given us a key so we could spend time in the house at any time if we wished.

As I referred to in Chapter 2, the week also gave both Jacqueline and I the chance to read a book that David Gelman loaned to us called "*The Jewish Way in Death and Mourning*" by Maurice Lamm. It was an exceptionally well (and simply) written book set out in a very logical order. The chapters were chronological with their titles being (1) From the moment of death to the funeral service, (2) The funeral service and the interment, (3) Mourning observances of Shiva and Sheloshim (periods of time post the death), (4) Yearlong mourning observances, (5) Post-mourning practices and procedures, (6) Special situations and (7) The world beyond the grave. It was outstanding in that it set out not only what would (or should) happen at each stage but also the origins of the actions/customs and the practical reasons for them i.e. the "what" and the "why". By reading that book during the week I felt I had a vastly improved understanding of what had/was happening and comfort that we were doing (and could continue to do) the right things over the coming weeks and months in memory of dad.

One of the customs for men was not to shave for the first month as a sign of respect (and also so that the focus would remain on the person lost, not on the appearance of the person grieving). It wasn't the first time I had sported a beard, having grown one way back in my sixth form days and through University. The beard grew quickly, but to my dismay not all of it was dark to match my hair colour. There were grey bits in some places. All of a sudden for the first time in my life I started to feel old, with the combination of losing both parents and this physical tell-tale sign etc.!

This time the week of mourning had a very different feel from the equivalent week when mum passed away. At that time, in addition to the initial shock, the focus and thoughts had been a lot around the future – looking after dad; what arrangements and changes would need to take place including medical aspects; all the practicalities we would face re moving dad down to Surrey and selling the house etc. Jacqueline was still working at that time and I was in transition having only just taken early retirement from British Airways. This time there was a real calmness over the period. There was nobody else to look after, no major moves or medical challenges faced us in the future and there was even a detailed, registered Will which would simplify the executorship of dad's estate. Also, Jacqueline was retired and I was only working two days a week (with no particular pressure to return to work quickly). Even in terms of reciting the prayer of mourning ("*Kaddish*") that was something we were both now familiar with (unfortunately). Consequently this gave much more time for reading (as mentioned above), understanding and reflection on the loss. This situation was created partly by the nature of Jewish custom (the period of "*Shiva*") and partly by the fact that it was the second parent who had passed away. However, on reflection I would recommend to anyone that in similar circumstances it would be beneficial to try and create some period of time, a "fire break", to draw breath and start to come to terms with the loss. Dashing back to work or headlong into dealing with administrative issues may not be the best approach in the long run (albeit I appreciate everyone's circumstances are different and we all deal with such loss in a personal way).

Finally, the last evening of prayers took place and on Sunday 25th November we drove back to Surrey. It was inevitable that there was an immense feeling of leaving something behind in Leeds and some trepidation about the adjustments we would have to make back in Surrey. 2012 had been all consuming, and increasingly intense, since dad's fall back in January. Now there wouldn't be the need to be visiting Laird Court virtually every day or the need to deal with the next major problem/medical challenge and that was going to feel extremely strange. It would take a long time to adjust to this new world. Also, hanging over us like the sword of Damacles, there would be the painful, emotional necessity to go into dad's bedroom with him no longer being there and go through all of his belongings (including all his clothes) at some stage and agree who would keep what, which items we would need to sell or give away etc. Some of the equipment such as the special bed, turntable etc., had to be returned sooner rather than later as unfortunately other people needed the same type of support as we had received.

I decided to take an extra day as compassionate leave on the Tuesday and didn't return to work until Thursday

29th November – my birthday. As you would expect, in the circumstances, this birthday was a very subdued affair as I was in no mood for celebrations. Also, facing people at work was not easy as they wished to express their condolences, but the situation was still too raw and recent to talk much about it without getting emotional. One saving grace was that the newly arrived beard didn't attract as much attention as normal, as there was the "*Movember*" charity event taking place that month and many people assumed that was the reason for the new growth.

I started to send letters and copies of the death certificate to various organisations that needed to know about dad's passing. I also arranged for his official Will to be retrieved from its storage location so we could initiate the probate process (as this may take some time). Charles Gibson, who was part of the firm Gibson Forge Associates, came over to the house once the Will had been received so that all the correct probate paperwork could be completed and sent off. It is really worth engaging a professional to help in these circumstances, as the use of a wrong form or incorrect completion can delay these matters substantially. Even for a relatively straight forward Will/estate as dad's was, we ended up having to send three forms, the death certificate, the Will and two copies and a covering letter, as well as the inevitable cheque, to the probate registry in Winchester!

One of the matters that Jacqueline and I discussed early on was that we wished to make donations to some of the people/organisations that had helped and supported dad in recent times. Also, we wanted to go and thank them personally for their help and support as obviously there had been no time to see any of them since the death. The first visit was in many ways the hardest, as it was to the Dialysis Centre in West Byfleet. This would be the first time we had been back there since that pivotal Friday at the beginning of November when dad had his last (partial) dialysis session. When we got to the centre we talked to Marion on reception and waited until some of the nursing staff had time to come out and meet us. Obviously we talked a bit about what had transpired and thanked them profusely for everything they had done for dad over the years (hugs and tears all round). We could see through the glass panes in the door into the main dialysis ward and I couldn't help looking to where dad's bed was – with someone else in it. I know Jacqueline did not want to go into the main part of the centre as she said she would find that too painful at this stage. We also took the opportunity to advise them about the donation we were going to make and obtain details of where to send the money. It would be earmarked specifically for that centre, not just going into a general pot to be spent. We would return to the centre one more time, the following week, in order to talk to Dr Marsh and thank him personally for everything he had done for us.

That visit was early on the following Tuesday morning, before Dr Marsh started his clinic there. We spent a few minutes with him and thanked him for his understanding, empathy and support throughout the many years dad had been under his care. We appreciated that it had been difficult for him at times and that he had been extremely flexible throughout to provide us with the best support in very difficult situations. He said it had been a pleasure and that it was so heart-warming to see such a strongly supportive and loving family as we had been. He had the greatest admiration for dad and thought he was an exceptional person. We also let him know of our donation as a practical token of thanks for everything – which he greatly appreciated. As we left he had a hug for the both of us – a sign of the close and mutually respective relationship we had built over the years.

Another visit we made was to see the Beacon (palliative care) nurses who had looked after dad in the latter stages, including providing the night nurse support. They were based over at Guildford and Jacqueline and I dropped over one afternoon at the end of the first week in December. Again, it was good to see them in less traumatic circumstances and express both our emotional and practical thanks. I must admit that these sessions were not easy as it necessitated talking about what had happened recently, thus re-opening still tender wounds. But maybe this was all part of the healing and acceptance process.

The other two visits and donations we made were in the last full week before Christmas. The first was a visit to Woking Hospice to visit Sarah Ivy, who had helped us through the last months and co-ordinated a lot of the support. She was based at the Hospice and we gave her our thanks and met one of the senior fundraisers for the Hospice who gratefully received our donation. The final donation was to Graham Pullen who ran A2B Ambulances who had looked after dad so well when he was bed bound and supported Jacqueline and I throughout. He dropped into Laird Court one afternoon in between jobs to spend time with us over a cup of tea and to receive our thanks.

One piece of advice is, wherever possible, to complete and sign a gift aid form for any charity you end up making a donation to. This allows them to claim back tax on the donation and increase the total amount received by the charity i.e. as a taxpayer if you donate £80 to a charity then they will be able to claim a further £20 back in tax, receiving £100 in total.

Christmas in 2012 was a very strange affair. I had always spent that time either with mum and dad up in Leeds, or with dad and Jacqueline (and Andreas) in Bagshot. For the first time in the twenty years since we met I would spend the time with Linda at her father's house in Taunton (along with her brother and nephew). In nearly sixty years this would be the first time that I couldn't spend that time with my parents. Linda's family made me very welcome over the festivities (as they always did generally when we visited) but obviously it was not the same. I would be saying "*Kaddish*" (the prayer of mourning) each day for a year (as custom required) and so each day there was that strong reminder of what I had lost. Sometimes I would sit on the settee and look across to the table where Linda and her brother and father were and I would start to well up – as all the memories started to flood back of the great Christmas's mum, dad, Jacqueline and I had spent together over the years. Although it was nice to be able to spend Christmas with Linda after so many years this couldn't compensate for the gaping hole that had appeared recently in my life.

We returned home to Surrey on 28th December and spent New Year's Eve having a meal out at The Inn @ West End, just a five minute walk around the corner from our house. As we walked back home around 11 o'clock that night I pondered on the *annus horribilis* that 2012 had been for us. The future would be very different from now on and I found this New Year's Eve a deflated and depressing time.

Chapter 10

After the extremes of 2012 both Jacqueline and I needed a break to recharge the batteries physically and start the mental healing process. She managed to get a very good deal on a transatlantic cruise to New York on Cunard's Queen Mary 2 departing from Southampton during the first few days of 2013. Linda and I decided to have a week's crash out in the Maldives. We first visited the islands back in March 2004, supposedly for a once in a lifetime trip, and were so blown away by the nearest thing to paradise we had visited that we returned the following year!! It was the ideal place just to do nothing and recharge a very tired body and mind. This time we stayed at the Olhuveli Beach Resort in South Male Atoll. The wonderful thing about the Maldives is the complete peace and quiet plus the stunning picture postcard islands with powder white sand and deep blue seas teeming with tropical fish. Although Linda offered me various books during my days relaxing on a sun lounger I always said no thanks. I just wanted to rest, sleep and let my mind take a break from the daily (or hourly) challenges I had faced with Jacqueline during the previous year. Certainly on returning home I felt much better physically, but it would take a long time for the mental recuperation to take place (something which is still not really complete to this day).

Whilst we were away the court approved probate for dad's estate which allowed me to tie up all the financial matters over the next two or three weeks – closing down all the bank and savings accounts, obtaining the appropriate tax refunds and finally splitting the value of the estate equally between Jacqueline and I. By the end of January I was able to tie up all these elements and set out the final statement. With having a correctly completed and registered Will the whole process had been able to be dealt with much quicker than when I had been attending to mum's estate post her death.

One of the remaining matters to deal with was agreeing on the headstone for dad and arranging the consecration ceremony for some time during the summer of 2013. Such ceremonies were not performed during the winter time due to the poor weather, but would normally be done within the first twelve months following the person's passing. We arranged the date for Sunday 28th July at 2 p.m. at the cemetery, followed by the unveiling of a plaque and refreshments back at Donisthorpe Hall in Leeds at 3 p.m. (the same as we had done for mum).

This time, in addition to the appropriate wording on the headstone, we also decided to have horizontal black granite stone slabs covering the whole of mum and dad's double grave, with a "Star of David" (shield to be historically correct) thereon and the simple wording across the complete width saying "May their souls rest together in eternal peace". The headstone would be very similar to mums and read:

"TREASURED MEMORIES OF
A DEVOTED HUSBAND AND FATHER
IAN MILES HARRIS
PASSED AWAY 16th NOVEMBER 2012
AGED 95 YEARS

DEEPLY MOURNED AND SADLY MISSED
BY HIS ADORING CHILDREN
JACQUELINE AND RUSSELL,
SON-IN-LAW, DAUGHTER-IN-LAW,
FAMILY AND FRIENDS

SHALOM".

We dealt with these immediate issues, but it would be some time until Jacqueline felt that she was up to going through dad's clothes and personal belongings with me. Although I fully understood those feelings there was some frustration on my part as I felt we had this cloud hanging over us for some months – knowing that it was something we would have to do at some point. However, everyone has a different emotional make-up and in these situations you can only move at the pace of the slowest person – you have to wait until they are ready to face such tasks, despite your own feelings. There is no defined or right time. However, my advice would be not to leave such tasks too long as otherwise their items could become a sort of shrine, which may not be helpful in the overall acceptance and healing process.

One of the things I had done after mum's passing was plant a rose bush in one of the borders in our back garden in her memory. There is an ornate stake next to it with a brass plate at the top simply saying "For

Mum – June 2006". When we were all living at the house on Harrogate Road in Leeds we had a rose bush in the back garden which had a wonderful perfume and deep red roses. Mum always used to love those roses and hence the reason for planting a similar rose bush after her death. I thought it would be appropriate to plant an equivalent rose bush in memory of dad close to mum's and did so in early 2013. Again it had a similar ornate stake and the annotation was "For Dad – November 2012".

One of the conclusions that I came to with some of the reflections I had in the months following dad's departure was the need to seize the day ("carpe diem"). Although I had travelled extensively throughout my life (in particular due to working for British Airways for so many years) there were still a number of places on the "we must do ...." list. I decided that instead of saying we must do those sometime I would write down this "bucket list" and we should consciously spend most of our holidays working through them while we were still fit enough to do so. Hence, the next trip we planned for the end of March was a nine day break that took us to Jordan. We were particularly keen to see the ancient Nabataean city of Petra as well as visiting the likes of the Dead Sea, Mt Nebo (where Moses ascended to view the land of Israel), the roman city of Jerash and Wadi Rum. During the rest of 2013 the main holidays comprised an Alaskan Cruise on Princess Cruise Line (in June) and a couple of weeks in Peru (September/ October), visiting Lima, the Sacred Valley, Machu Picchu, Cuzco and Lake Titicaca. We also managed long weekends away in Florence (May) and Israel (November – which I will return to later on as there was a particular significance to that trip) and a day trip to Marseille for Linda's birthday in February.

Ever since her mum passed away in 2009, Linda had always gone down to see her father in Taunton once a month (and her brother did the same, so there was someone visiting and helping him every couple of weeks). During 2012 I had stopped going down with her due to the full time commitment needed with dad, but now the situation had changed I started accompanying her each month and helping out wherever possible (doing the driving to take the strain off her as she was working full time, mowing the back lawn at her dad's etc.). Also there was now time to consider other things. We had been talking about getting a new television and also changing our PC as it was a few years old and going at an increasingly slow pace despite care and attention! There was now time to go around to different shops and research what was available/what we might want, so during the first quarter of 2013 a new flat screen television finally replaced the big, old, cathode ray Sony set and also the office (in our third bedroom) finally acquired a new, fast HP PC with a 23 inch flat screen – the joys of modern technology!

In 2013 the remembrance of mum's passing ("*Yahrzeit*") fell in late May, so we made arrangements to mark this in Leeds during the last weekend in May. We made it an extended weekend, going up on the Friday and returning Monday afternoon. The main focus was the visit to the synagogue (implanted in Donisthorpe Hall) on the Saturday morning followed by a "*Kiddush*" for the congregation (paid for by us) in memory of mum afterwards. The long weekend gave us the chance to spend time with various friends and family – the first time since we had come up for dad's funeral back in November the previous year.

It also gave us the opportunity to visit one of dad's oldest friends from his teaching days – Geoff Wilson. Geoff had come down to Surrey for dad's 90th birthday a few years before despite the fact that he was not significantly younger than dad. He lived on his own just outside Leeds and although he was still driving he was finding getting around increasingly difficult. As mentioned previously, we had bought dad a mobility scooter as a present a few years earlier. It was the type that could be taken apart and carried in the boot of a car, then re-assembled quickly when the destination was reached. Despite dad using it a number of times it was still in pristine condition. Jacqueline had been in contact with Geoff Wilson and had indicated that, if it would be of use to him, she and I would like him to have the scooter (we were sure dad would have wanted the same). He was very grateful and wanted to pay us for it but we refused on more than one occasion – we were just happy that it would go to a good home and be of use. We took time out during this visit to Leeds to go over to Geoff's, spend some time with him and deliver his new "toy"!

In between this weekend and departing on the Alaskan Cruise in mid-June we had the pleasure of a visit from Marcia Haskin from Australia. She had been on a cruise prior to ending up in London and it was good to see her. It had been a while since she had been over last and despite talking to people on the telephone from time to time it is no substitute for getting together in person. She was staying at the Mayfair Hotel on Stratton Street in London and both Jacqueline and I had the opportunity to spend time with her during her short stay.

No sooner had we returned from the cruise in late June than thoughts turned to the final arrangements for the consecration of dad's headstone in Leeds at the end of July. We arranged for a notification to go in the Jewish Telegraph paper in Leeds for a couple of consecutive weeks. Letting people know what was happening and the time/location etc. Also I had compiled a short synopsis of dad's life and arranged for this to be passed to whoever would be officiating at the ceremony, so they could talk about dad's life and achievements accordingly. This time when we were up in Leeds we would also get the chance to see a further memorial we had paid for at Donisthorpe Hall. They had decided to create a "Memories of Life" tree in the courtyard just off the main reception area of the Hall. This was a twelve foot high artificial tree, with copper leaves that could be purchased and inscribed with the name(s) of loved ones and dates if you wished. We decided to purchase a leaf and have the names and dates for both mum and dad inscribed. The unveiling of the tree took place in mid-June, so our visit at the end of July would be the first opportunity to see it.

Before this visit though, Jacqueline and I made a trip to just outside Birmingham to take part in the graduation celebrations of Moira's daughter Hadassah. She was qualifying as a doctor after five years studying at Birmingham University. She always got on well with mum and dad when she was living across the road from their flat in Primley Park Garth. Moira would often send her and her brother (Jesse) over to give dad a hand getting the food shopping out of his car and up to the first floor flat when he had been down to Sainsbury's. Also, as she got older, dad would take time to discuss her academic progress and give thoughts and advice on what she might pursue as a career. Although we were not able to attend the actual graduation ceremony (limited seating) we took part in the (barbeque) celebrations back at the house where she and her boyfriend were living at the time. It seemed a little strange emotionally as we were there in our own rights, but also as if we were representing mum and dad. When Hadassah returned from the ceremony I gave her a hug and congratulated her – and also said that dad would have been very proud of her. I always remember that this brought tears to her eyes as she had always been very fond of him.

Just before the consecration weekend Jacqueline and I had to make a flying (literally) visit to Leeds for a cremation. One of dad's cousins – Maurice Bailey – had died. Although he was Jewish he didn't really follow the religion and therefore had decided he wished to be cremated rather than buried. Maurice was a good friend of mum and dad's having visited them at the flat in Leeds many times. Also, after mum's passing, he often used to drive out to the Holiday Inn at Garforth to meet up with dad (and us) when we came up for any reason. We all used to sit in the lounge area having a tea or coffee catching up with everything. Again the memory of a vision that could no longer be repeated! With both Jacqueline and I having our (retired) staff travel concessions we could get very reasonable tickets on British Midland, who flew from Heathrow to Leeds/Bradford Airport. As we were only going to be up for the day it saved a lot of driving – with a 7:55 a.m. flight up and then an evening flight back. Our cousin Leslie arranged to pick us up at the airport and drop us back there in the evening.

It was a hectic week, as four days later we found ourselves driving back up to Leeds for the consecration. That was on the Sunday at 2 p.m. followed by the unveiling of a plaque at the synagogue in Donisthorpe Hall and refreshments there from 3 p.m. On the Saturday, after attending the normal morning service at the synagogue, Linda and I decided to drive over to Harrogate for a walk around and afternoon tea. Neither of us had ever gone into the famous "Betty's" tearoom there (established in 1919), so we decided it was an experience long overdue!

This enjoyable episode was in stark contrast to the solemn affairs of the Sunday. There was a congregation of about thirty people who met at the cemetery that afternoon. Just before the start of the prayers Jacqueline said to me that she had written something that she would like to say afterwards (in addition to the details of dad's life I had typed up and passed to those officiating). I was surprised she hadn't mentioned it much earlier, but afterwards she said she didn't know whether she would feel up to delivering it on the day. Despite the months having passed I am not sure I would have trusted myself to being able to say such heartfelt words at the time without breaking down.

As usual there were the prayers, words about dad from those officiating and Jacqueline and then we all moved outside to the graveside. Again, there was a cloth covering the whole of the double headstone. Once this was removed it revealed the matching elements and wording for mum and dad. At last the whole site had the appropriate completeness and the quality that mum and dad deserved. The black, granite, shining double headstone was all beautifully inscribed in gold lettering and the width of the double grave covered by equivalent black granite horizontal slabs with the inscription we had agreed. It was a fitting memorial to two amazingly wonderful people. The final prayers were said by us at the graveside and the ceremony concluded. Once most of the congregation had disbursed I did take the opportunity to take a couple of photos with the camera I had slipped in my pocket so I would always have a record of this pristine memorial.

We gradually made our way back to Donisthorpe Hall and the ceremony for the unveiling of the memorial plaque was carried out. Ironically, the person who carried out the ceremony happened to be a man called Andrew Tunick – he and I had been in the same class together at Roundhay Grammar School and used to play football together there on a regular basis (he did mention this in his address – which made the ceremony that much more personal). After that everyone retired to enjoy the refreshments we had provided and catch up generally. It also gave us the opportunity to go and see the leaf on the "Memories of Life" tree in the courtyard. Jacqueline and Andreas drove back to London that afternoon, but Linda and I had decided to stay an extra day in Leeds and return on the Monday.

Linda and I were both back at work on the Tuesday. Since the beginning of July I had increased my working days from two to three per week (normally Tuesday to Thursday). After dad's passing Linda and I had discussed our plans for the future quite a bit and how long each of us would continue to work (and how many days a week). Having done the "financial sums" we had decided that I would increase my days to three per week for around eighteen months and then retire (again) when I hit sixty – I was fifty eight at the time. We also agreed that Linda would look to work four days a week rather than five (if possible) until she was fifty eight (another five years). Having discussed various projects and opportunities with my boss at Monitor the three days a week worked well as there was a particular project coming up (relating to the licencing of Independent Providers to the NHS) that I could be part of three days a week, whereas just two days a week would probably not be enough time. Linda managed to get agreement from her boss to generally work four days a week (Friday off) on an informal basis, albeit she would need to go in on certain Friday's if one of her colleague's was on leave or off ill.

The summer of 2013 passed without great incident – a real contrast to the previous year. Jacqueline and I had one get together at the beginning of August where we went through some of dad's boxes that had been stored away and never unpacked. It would be much later in the year before we finally got around to going through his personal possessions.

As I had experienced after mum's passing, the first year of events often brought back heightened emotions. That was inevitable, especially when we arrived at dad's birthday on 16th October. The mind wandered back to the situation the previous year (which was a very painful time anyway) and previous, more enjoyable birthdays and celebrations. There was no need to rack our brains this year as to what presents to get dad (who invariably used to say he didn't really need anything). Oh what I would have given to have that headache again this year.

Also visiting places that we had taken dad to often prompted painful feelings, especially the first time round. I particularly remember dropping into the Longacres garden centre near us over the summer. After doing the shopping we needed to do Linda and I decided to stop off in their café and have a bite to eat and a drink. As we sat there my gaze moved across to an empty table where we had sat with dad for the last time the previous year. I could almost see the ghostly picture of the past with him slumped in his wheelchair in so much pain – and then the vision, like so much else, faded away. My eyes welled up with tears and Linda just held my hand, knowing what I was thinking and going through.

Similar emotions were never far beneath the surface, whether it be visiting Frimley Park Hospital, days out in Poole or Birdworld, or visits to Leeds – they all resounded with the echoes of dad and the times we had spent together in those places. Although such under-tones will probably always remain to some extent, they do seem to fade somewhat and become less intense as time passes.

The first anniversary of dad's passing seemed to come around very quickly. In 2013 it fell on Tuesday 5th November, so we arranged to have the remembrance thereof in the synagogue on the previous Saturday morning (2nd November). I might not have explained earlier that the annual anniversary ("*Yahrzeit*") is always based on the Jewish date of death and the Jewish calendar.

The Jewish year is not the same length as a solar year on the civil calendar used by most of the western world, so the date shifts on the civil calendar.

The Jewish calendar is based on three astronomical phenomena: the rotation of the Earth about its axis (a day); the revolution of the moon about the Earth (a month); and the revolution of the Earth about the sun (a year). These three phenomena are independent of each other, so there is no direct correlation between them. On average, the moon revolves around the Earth in about 29½ days. The Earth revolves around the sun in about 365¼ days, that is, about 12.4 lunar months.

The civil calendar (Gregorian calendar in the western world) used by most of the world has abandoned any correlation between the moon cycles and the month, arbitrarily setting the length of months to 28, 30 or 31 days.

The Jewish calendar, however, coordinates all three of these astronomical phenomena. Months are either 29 or 30 days, corresponding to the 29½-day lunar cycle. Years are either 12 or 13 months, corresponding to the 12.4 month solar cycle. To compensate for this "drift", the Jewish calendar uses a 12-month lunar calendar with an extra month occasionally added. Hence, although mum and dad's dates of death are obviously fixed in the Jewish calendar, they move around each year in terms of the civil calendar. Also the year number on the Jewish calendar represents the number of years since creation, calculated by adding up the ages of people in the Bible back to the time of creation. Hence, mum passed away in 5766 and dad in 5773.

There had been some issues with the catering facilities (and renovations thereto) at Donisthorpe Hall in Leeds so Jacqueline and I finally decided to have the remembrance "*Kiddush*" this time at a more local synagogue that Jacqueline was now attending in Staines. They had the ability to put on a much more extensive (and fitting) spread after the Saturday morning service

– with open roll sandwiches, cakes, fish balls etc., etc. Generally in Leeds they had only been able to supply a basic biscuit and cake offering. Again, these events were always somewhat emotional in nature. There was the need to recite the prayer of mourning again within the service and the person taking the service would usually make some address covering the deceased person etc. However, it did bring a certain comforting feeling that we were doing everything possible to remember (mum and dad) and pay them the vast respect they deserved.

At the end of November Linda and I had arranged to have a long weekend away over the period of my birthday (which fell on Friday 29th November). However, this would not be a normal celebration weekend but would have particular significance. The plan was to visit Israel and make our way to the Western Wall in Jerusalem. I would then say prayers of mourning for both mum and dad, as the ultimate sign of respect to them.

Most religions have physical sites that are of paramount importance. For Judaism probably the most holy place is deemed to be the Western Wall (often referred to as the "Wailing Wall") in Jerusalem. It is a relatively small segment of the structure which originally composed the western retaining wall of the Second Jewish Temple atop the hill known as the Temple Mount to Jews and Christians. The Temple Mount is the holiest site in Judaism and is the place to which Jews turn during prayer, and the Western Wall is considered holy due to its connection to the Temple. Due to the ban on praying on the Mount, the Wall is the holiest place where Jews are permitted to pray. The original, natural and irregular-shaped Temple Mount was gradually extended to allow for an ever larger Temple compound to be built at its top. This process was finalised by Herod the Great, who enclosed the Mount with an almost rectangular set of retaining walls, built to support extensive substructures and earth fills needed to give the natural hill a geometrically regular shape. On top of this box-like structure Herod built a vast paved esplanade which surrounded the Temple. Of the four retaining walls, the western one is considered to be closest to the former Temple, which makes it the most sacred site recognised by Judaism outside the former Temple Mount esplanade.

We flew out to Tel Aviv on my birthday and had the rest of Friday and Saturday relaxing and sightseeing around Tel Aviv. I had visited Israel many years before with mum, dad and Jacqueline (we stayed at the Hilton on the sea front in Tel Aviv), but Linda had never been there before. This time we were staying at the Sheraton Hotel which was just a short distance away from the Hilton on the sea front. We were fortunate to have glorious sunny weather throughout the long weekend.

On Sunday we had booked an excursion to Jerusalem and I had checked that we would have enough free time for me to say the prayers I wanted to at the wall. It was an interesting trip generally, as I had a chance to contrast how a lot of the areas outside Old Jerusalem had changed over the years. The journey also epitomised the changes, in that the modern motorway/dual carriageway roads sped us to Jerusalem in nearly half the time it had taken all those years before.

The time at the Western Wall was virtually at the end of our tour around Old Jerusalem (having followed the Stations of the Cross, visited the Church of the Holy Sepulche and had a refreshment break/time for some shopping). We had about twenty minutes free time at the wall and I took out my prayer shawl and skull cap that I had brought with and made my way down to the side of the wall. I said the prayer of mourning ("*Kaddish*") for both mum and dad and also for neighbours of mum and dad's in Leeds (Lou and Pearl Stoller) who had recently passed away. There is somewhat of a tradition in that people also write messages on small pieces of paper, fold them up and put them into the cracks of the wall. I had decided to do the same on my visit and took out what I had written for mum and dad, folded it up and placed it carefully into a crack in the wall. I then walked slowly back to meet up with Linda. We just stood there holding each other as I again fought back the tears – it seemed to be the end of a very long journey. As we came away from Jerusalem I did feel a sense of calmness – probably as most people feel when they have finally done something they were determined to do. It seemed a fitting end to a chapter in my life and something I am sure mum and dad would have appreciated.

On the same excursion we then went on to Bethlehem before returning to Tel Aviv. To get there you have to go by foot across the border crossing (as it is in the Palestinian Territory on the West Bank). On a slightly more light-hearted note, we had no problem going across, but on trying to return they nearly didn't want to let Linda back into Israel! It hadn't been made clear that security would want to actually see our passports. Fortunately I had a photocopy I had taken of mine along with my driving licence as ID, but Linda just had her driving licence. There was no problem going out of Israel but on our return they took a very firm line with Linda. Despite showing what ID she had they were still not inclined to let her back in! Eventually I remembered that I had taken photos of each of our passports on my smartphone, so brought this up and showed it to the crossing guards (explaining again that the original was back in our hotel in Tel Aviv and obviously that had been checked on our arrival into Tel Aviv on the Friday). Eventually I think they took pity on Linda, as (a) she was not on her own and (b) really didn't look like a terrorist of any sort, so they grudgingly decided to let us through – a close call. We flew home to "welcoming" Blighty the next day.

It wasn't long until Christmas came around and for the second time both Linda and I made our way down to her dad's in Taunton for the festive period, returning just before New Year.

Chapter 11

The last couple of years (2014 and 2015) have been a gradual period of change and adjustment – a process which is still slow and ongoing.

There are now the regular *"Yahrzeits"* (anniversaries) for mum and dad around June and November each year, plus the occasional visits to Leeds to see family and friends. These visits always include a visit to the cemetery to visit mum and dad's grave. We have had some restoration work done recently at the cemeteries in Leeds to restore the gravestones for both mum's parents (something she was keen to do whilst she was alive, but never had the opportunity to complete) and for my great aunt's grave (Auntie Ray). We held the *"Kiddush"* for dad in November 2014 back in Leeds and it gave us the opportunity to present two engraved silver goblets to the synagogue in memory of mum and dad. We had come across these whilst going through dad's items and I had arranged for them to be engraved accordingly with mum and dad's names and dates.

Other changes in 2014 included my decision to end my leisure flying after nearly thirty years. I had obtained my Private Pilots' Licence (PPL) way back in the 1980's and had flown Piper Tomahawks and Warriors from the BA Flying Club based at Wycombe Air Park ever since.

However, with the age of sixty looming and the increase in the amount of flying needed to retain the licence and keep up with the "recency" rules it seemed the right time to let my recency lapse. My last flight touched down at Wycombe Air Park on 15 March 2014.

With the changes that had happened Linda and I finally got around to revising and updating our Wills during the early part of 2014. It is something that is easy to put off, but brings a certain peace of mind once it is done. I kept pushing Jacqueline along the same lines, as she had never made a Will, and I'm pleased to say that early 2015 saw her Will finally in place. I was talking to our good friends Hazel and Jim recently and they have gone a step further, not only having up to date Wills but also having arranged lasting power of attorneys for both of them, to cover the possible scenario of finding themselves in the situation where one (or both) of them were to become incapable of making decisions (financial and general). It is a good idea to take these steps whilst you are capable, as it is all too easy to stick your head in the sand and take the "I'm fine now; I'll deal with it if it happens" attitude – invariably too late!

The "bucket list" holidays continued for Linda and I during 2014, with main holidays including a Baltic Cruise (including St. Petersburg) and an extensive visit to Japan in the autumn, interlaced with short breaks to Abu Dhabi, Gibraltar and Porto. One sobering aspect of these was the fact that I always used to look forward to coming home and taking mum and dad through the photos and experiences – something that was no longer possible. Although Jacqueline and I go through the photos it's not quite the same any more.

I also remember having to adjust the pre-printed address list I used to send postcards whilst on holiday to take dad's name off it.

Jacqueline and I did start to go through dad's personal effects from late on in 2013. This took quite a while as we felt that an hour or two at a time was enough. This is probably one of the most personal things that needs to be done when someone close passes away and there are no rights or wrongs – people should do it when they feel up to it and for as long or short a period as they feel up to at the time. These sessions were quite often emotional as you would expect. Surprisingly, it was not always the obvious items that triggered the strong emotions but it could be small items with particular significance or of a very personal nature (spectacles, hearing aids etc.). The clothes were in many ways the easiest set of items to go through. I had decided I wished to keep one of a number of items (shirt, cardigan, trousers, coat and bow tie – the latter being dad's "signature" look). Jacqueline also kept certain items and we agreed that the remainder would all be taken up to Leeds and given to the Jewish Welfare Board to help people in need.

We managed to agree a split of certain other key items without too much difficulty (and a reasonable amount of give and take). This included a collection of around 130 spoons. I had started to bring these back for mum from my trips with British Airways back in the 1980's and it had snowballed over the years with Jacqueline then starting to do the same (and a few other people likewise). It was an impressive collection with all the different country designs and emblems and we had acquired display cases which had been hung all around dad's bedroom at Laird Court. It was always something he took great pride in, telling people how many he had and some of the exotic places they had come from. Half of the display cases and spoons now reside at my house and the other half remain displayed at Jacqueline's in what was dad's bedroom.

Even today we have not finished dealing with all of dad's belongings. We have been through everything once, agreed the split of various items, agreed which other items we should probably give away or dispose of and quite a lot of items that probably should be sold as appropriate (through auctions, dealers and the like). It is very much this last set that remain to be finally dealt with at some stage.

Another adjustment that has taken place is the frequency of contact between Jacqueline and I. The crises with mum and dad naturally threw us together on a daily basis for a number of years. Prior to that we were always in touch, but not on a daily/regular basis. Post mum and dad leaving us the necessity for regular contact has diminished (especially after various matters have been dealt with, as set out previously in this book). It is probably natural now that we only have contact around once a week, with one of us dropping in to see the other and spend time catching up fairly regularly, but like everything else this takes some adjustment to come to terms with.

During 2014 there were a couple of milestones that took place. The first was in September, when my cousin Leslie's mother-in-law (Freya) reached her 100th birthday in Leeds. This had been touch and go earlier in the year when she fell at home and had been in hospital for some time. However, Leslie and Freya's extensive family put on a major celebration in Leeds on Sunday 14th September. Linda and I went up for the weekend and attended on the Sunday evening, which was very enjoyable. It is amazing, and still fairly rare, for anyone to reach 100 (with a letter from the Queen), but also it did trigger some reflections on my part – as both mum and dad had done well to make it into their nineties. The contrast that weekend was probably the most extreme you can get – visiting mum and dad's graves at the cemetery on the Sunday morning and then celebrating the life of a centenarian in the evening. It does bring home the seemingly arbitrary nature of life and death, why some people pass away early, others at 91 and 95 and others are still with us after a hundred years.

At the end of November, the other milestone was my 60th birthday. Despite many suggestions I really didn't feel in the mood for a big party. The loss of mum and dad still hung over me even a couple of years after dad's passing (and eight year's after mum's departure). I decided that a more enjoyable and meaningful option would be to have a dinner together with a few invited close friends at Foxhills. Foxhills is a 400 acre resort with a listed Manor House, built in 1841, standing at its heart (with a 2 Rosette Restaurant) located in Ottershaw, Surrey. A lovely lounge area allows people to meet up and relax with a pre-dinner drink and peruse the menu, before going through to the Manor Restaurant with its vaulted ceiling and traditional open fireplace. After the meal you can retire back to the lounge area to have coffee and talk away the rest of the evening. There were ten of us in total (including Linda and I) and afterwards we adjourned back to our house in West End for champagne and birthday cake.

As part of my weekend of celebrations (or was it commiserations?) Linda booked to take me to Claridge's hotel in London for traditional afternoon tea on the Sunday. Again, a very indulgent afternoon, but something quieter and more civilised than a loud party. In the past birthdays and specific ages did not particularly bother me, but since mum and dad's departures they have had a more downbeat and depressing effect on me generally. It is the constant reminder of the inevitable passage of time and the thoughts of the issues that older age will no doubt throw up. In a similar vein both Linda and I had been having the annual winter flu jabs for some years. I think it started with looking after dad, to minimise the possibility that one of us might catch something and then pass it on to Ian with being in such regular close contact. Also, with Linda's father being in his eighties the same logic applied.

The specific milestone of sixty also brought reflections on the speed that life seemed to be passing. Your own mortality suddenly seems to feature more overtly in your thoughts (and the fear that can instil) and there is a realisation of potentially how few years might remain compared with those experienced to date. In the past my mind-set had generally been that of looking forward to future potential achievements and the enjoyable experiences that (hopefully) life would offer. I had been fortunate in generally having a fit and healthy life over the years, always having played sports and been a regular user of a sports/health club over the years. Even when any illness or health problem arose my attitude had always been that of expecting it to be cured or rectified to a large extent and that it was only going to be a temporary problem. Now I find that when issues arise I have a more negative mind-set, wondering whether this is going to be something that is either (a) more severe, and/or (b) something that I might have to live with rather than it being cured or rectified. I try to switch into my previous, more optimistic modus-operandi, but I think the years of seeing mum and dad suffer from various issues and illnesses (and their associated deterioration) has embedded a more negative viewpoint into my thinking. This can be another side-effect of personal loss and one which people may not identify so obviously. At least it is something I am now aware of and can try to address and tackle going forward.

The other element of fear arises from the fact that neither Linda nor I have any children. I look to how much support and care Jacqueline and I provided to mum and dad in the latter years and realise that there are not any equivalent people who might be able to provide us with the same sort of support should we need it in similar circumstances – not a comforting thought.

Towards the end of 2014 brought confirmation of my decision to give up regular work around the age of sixty. I had discussed the exact timing with Paul Streat, my boss at Monitor, for some time and was originally thinking of the end of 2014. However, given what was happening with the work I was involved in (NHS Foundation Trusts that had been placed into "Special Measures" due to quality issues) I agreed to carry on until March 2015 to finish off various elements of the role. So, in December 2014, I finally gave in my official notice (which was a three month period) so I knew I would be leaving on 31st March. This was in line with Linda and my "grand plan" that we had agreed after dad passed away. In fact it would mean I had worked a little longer than we had originally planned. All being well we are still looking for Linda to stop working when she hits fifty eight in just over a couple of years' time.

Stopping work has been yet another major change in my life and I am still adjusting to the "next phase". Over the first few months it gave me the time to do most of those jobs you always put off, such as staining the garden shed, painting the surrounds of the garage, sorting masses of old paperwork and files etc. Probably the biggest benefit so far has been the time it has provided for me to finally plan and write this book! The adjustment will still take some time. Particularly if you have been blessed with a successful career, as I have, the transition can be difficult. You no longer have the "badge" of what you do for work. Your goals no longer include the next promotion or area of work you aspire to. Now when you meet new people the answer to the usual question – "what do you do" no longer trips off the tongue as "I'm a Senior Finance Manager at British Airways" or "I'm a Senior Manager at Monitor" – you have to think how to explain your early retirement and what you are now doing!

It is one of the challenges of later life that a number of things you have worked for, lived with and taken for granted for so long suddenly stop or disappear – your work, hobbies (such as flying) and your close family (such as parents). It is a wider plethora of loss than just the obvious passing of parents. Albeit not to the same extent as the latter, all these "losses" need to be attended to in their own ways. You need to appreciate them, come to terms with the change, grieve for them accordingly and then place them into their appropriate slot in your life and move on to the future keeping them as (hopefully) good memories from the past.

That has been one of the big challenges I have faced with losing mum and dad. For a long time my memories have been overwhelmed by the negative aspects of their lives – the times of their suffering and the painful final periods of their lives and passing. In terms of the myriad of memories I have of them over the years these, relatively, short periods seem to overwhelm the memory banks and blot out the good times. In the early periods after each of them died I would find it extremely difficult to talk about them without being overwhelmed by emotion – the scars were too raw and painful. Over time though I have come to be able to talk more freely about them and our experiences together as a family. Looking at some of the photos or DVD's on occasions starts to surface and re-assert all the positive times we spent together as a family. You slowly start to make the transition from the initial painful period into one where you realise that talking about such (good) times is a way to help their memories live on and is a type of celebration of their lives. Certainly I would table the advice for anyone to ensure they have some live video footage of a loved one during "normal"/good times. The ability to actually see and hear them as they were can be comforting at a later stage and provides a different level of memory and closeness from simple still photos.

Apart from stopping working in 2015 there have been some other challenges in relation to Linda's father. We had a period of two or three months when he was suddenly unwell and had to be taken into hospital urgently on two occasions within a period of about five weeks. At the moment (coming up to his 89th birthday) he seems in reasonable health given his age, but those periods earlier this year certainly brought back uncomfortable memories. At least going forward Linda and I have the experience of what happened to Fay and Ian to fall back on if we are faced with similar issues with her dad (albeit the 125 mile distance between us is certainly not a helpful factor).

On a positive note the ticking off of the "bucket list" regarding our travels has (fortunately) continued this year with main holidays to Doha (Qatar) – before the build up to the 2022 World Cup changes it out of all recognition – Zambia, to visit the Victoria Falls, and a cruise through the Panama Canal (as well as long weekends to the Algarve and Marrakesh).

One of the challenges that still faces me is the acceptance that the defined set of memories that comprise mum's life and dad's life are finite and complete. It is not that easy to explain, but it is the reflection that any major event that happens in the world now is part of my life and my memories – it makes up who Russell Harris is. However, they are no longer reflected in Ian or Fay's lives – the memory cards of their existence are complete and full; nothing else can be written to those. As an example, my 60th birthday celebrations were not part of their lives; they were not part of what Ian Harris and Fay Harris's lives were – they stopped in 2012 and 2006 respectively.

As we come up to the third year since dad slipped away from us I find the frequency of my thinking about him and mum has subsided and stabilised from the peak, painful times of the past. There has been some amelioration in my coping with the infinite loss, but that journey is far from over, as I will reflect on in the last chapter of this book. There are some words from a song called "*Wake me up when September ends*", written by the group Green Day back in 2004 which capture some of my feelings at this time. The lead singer Billie Jo Armstrong had lost his father a few years before and he expressed his feelings as follows:

"Like my father's come to pass,
Seven years has gone so fast,
Wake me up when September ends.

Here comes the rain again,
Falling from the stars,
Drenched in my pain again, becoming who we are.

As my memory rests,
But never forgets what I lost,
Wake me up when September ends".

The last few lines are probably the most poignant and appropriate for me at this time. You can never forget what has happened and what you have lost, as it has had and continues to have the most profound effect on your life, but your memory does rest at times and allows you to carry on with what remains of your own life.

Epilogue

The previous chapters have chronicled a period of my life spanning around ten years with the focus being on the loss of both my parents, the challenges that presented and the roller coaster of emotions experienced. By its nature it is a very personal and subjective view and portrayal of events during that time. If my sister, Jacqueline, was writing a similar book it would probably contain a lot of what I have imparted here, but with a unique view, and slant from her perspective and emotional impact. No two people would ever write the same book, no matter how close they were to a situation or how common the events they had experienced. That is something worth bearing in mind should you find yourself in a similar situation, coping with such pain and events with family members. As I mentioned at the beginning of this journey, the feelings and effects are unique to each of us as individuals, but the type of events suffered are global and universal.

Before I go on with more generic reflections, thoughts and advice I must take time out to heap praise on one person in particular – Jacqueline. Although there was support and help from other family, friends and acquaintances during these difficult times her love, support and fierce dedication to looking after mum and dad during the most difficult periods of their lives cannot be overstated. At many times it was above and beyond what could reasonably be expected of anyone in similar circumstances. At the extremes of our trials and tribulations when even I started to question things and felt I might waver her amazing resilience and single mindedness would re-energise me to take a deep breath, re-group and push on as required. That resilience was a trait that pervaded dad's life in particular and the determination to do the right thing no matter what the physical or emotional cost was something we both inherited from mum and dad. In a similar vein, dad's resoluteness and strength of mind to face the extreme traumas he faced in the last few years of his life, without ever complaining and virtually never losing his amazing sense of humour characterised a role model that we should all aspire to.

As I have touched on earlier in this book, I am sure many people do occasionally ponder on the potential timing of losing their parents. The easy answer is that there is no "best time" to lose a parent. Each timespan throws up its own pros and cons. In terms of a sibling's age when they lose a parent, like most things, this would probably follow a normal distribution (or bell curve). If they pass during your mid-life years then the time they have been with you is reduced and there is the downside of them missing out on sharing your achievements later in life. On the other hand, as an individual, you have more things to look forward to, such as family, career success etc., which may help ameliorate the feeling of loss. Obviously, should you be much older when they pass (as has been the case for Jacqueline and I) you can take the comfort of them having been with you for much longer and shared more events in your life – however, the ability to look to the future and potentially positive events to help abrogate some of the loss is much more limited. On a personal basis, maybe it is because I come in the latter category that I am struggling to come to terms with the losses and keep a more positive attitude going forward.

Also, the effect of a loss is different for each parent. You would tend to think that the effects and acceptance cycle when you lose your second parent would be similar to when you lost the first one. After all you have been through that experience once and life generally teaches you that experience of a situation helps you cope better with it the second time around. However, in this type of situation this is not so (from my experience). I anticipated that the loss of dad would be a mirror event in most ways to that when mum passed away, but they proved to be very different scenarios. It is worth being prepared, as far as anyone can be, for this differentiation along with the emotional implications. I probably missed the obvious difference in that the second scenario means that *neither* of the two people who created you will be around any longer, whereas in the first scenario there was one loss with one person still there to share feelings and experiences with (and who could become even more of a focus for your attentions).

Also, with one parent still alive there is still the background generic assumption that there is someone between yourself and the inevitable end, whereas with the second parent passing there is the sudden realisation that you are probably the "next in line" – this latter feeling can have profound effects on your state of mind and attitudes as you start to face the reality of your own mortality (maybe for the first time in earnest). There are also the practical differences between the two situations. With one parent still alive you have the opportunity to delve into the past and ask about people or events that you are not clear about. With both gone that "Wikipedia" of knowledge disappears and over time you realise that various questions can now never be answered or clarified (which adds to the sense of loss). The inference of that revelation is obvious, albeit not always easy to adopt – ask people about the past whenever the thought arises. Don't put it off to sometime in the future, as that time may be taken away.

I would like to turn to some of the individual challenges that Jacqueline and I faced over the period of this story and try and broaden them out into generic advice that the reader might find beneficial. At the peak of trying to deal with such situations as I've laid out in this book I don't believe it is particularly beneficial to try and look at the medium or long term. Sometimes, in the midst of such a maelstrom, it is necessary to just think short term in nature – hour to hour or day to day. You have to deal with and address the immediate problem or crisis you are faced with in the best way possible to restore as much stability into the situation as possible. If, having dealt with that, there is time to draw breath then that is the time to start considering the medium or longer term implications of the situation you are facing. Having said that, it is very easy to be too enveloped in just dealing with the short term and not assessing whether the situation is likely to continue for some considerable time (or even ad-infinitum). If the latter is likely the approach used to deal with the short term may prove unsustainable longer term – and therefore a change in approach to care and support (possibly with outside/additional help) may be required.

In the midst of the "hell" (as it sometimes seems) it is also important to try and take care of yourself as much as possible – both mentally and physically. At the end of the day, if a person is primarily relying on you for their care, then you becoming ill or incapable of continuing will also be detrimental for them as well. It is important to "manufacture" breaks as far as practical on a regular basis; to create some time for yourself. These need not necessarily be holidays or lengthy breaks, but maybe just a few hours to allow you to step out of the situation and take off the mantle of responsibility for a short time. This return to normality for short periods can help sustain you through what may prove to be an extended period of responsibility. It may be as simple as a few hours shopping, a walk around a garden centre and a stop for refreshments etc. Counter intuitively work may also be beneficial in certain circumstances. In my case I was only working two days a week towards the latter part of dad's life, but those short periods of time helped restore a certain amount of reality into my life. Too higher work demands would obviously be detrimental during periods of personal stress, but some level of work may prove beneficial as described above.

Exercising both the mind and body can also be helpful, if possible. Physically a work out at a gym or health club helps (and also helps clear your head as well) and some people may find that a short spell of meditation once or twice a day helps calm and settle your mind and emotions. These sessions do not need to be lengthy, even a ten or fifteen minute break can be restorative. On a practical level support from another person can be essential to seeing you through such tumultuous times. I was fortunate that there was two of us heavily involved in looking after mum and dad (Jacqueline and I) and even if there is just one primary carer some sort of arrangements should be worked out to provide some support and alleviation as much as possible – otherwise the primary carer may fall ill themselves. I was also extremely fortunate to have such a supportive wife in Linda – not only on an emotional level but also in practical terms. She ended up taking care of most things at home and also took the weight off me by dealing with all sorts of practical matters day to day, so that I could concentrate on supporting dad and Jacqueline as much as possible.

One piece of advice, as you go through such experiences, is to try and not dwell on key moments in the past – the "hindsight" situation – and beat yourself up over them. I agree that increased experience and knowledge gives you the ability to make different decisions when faced with a similar situation should it arise again. It is very easy to look back and say that you should have taken a different course of action regarding a person's care at a particular juncture. However, you only had a certain knowledge and experience (or not) at that time. As long as you can face yourself and genuinely say that given the facts at the time you made the best choice you could, with the best outcome in mind (given your knowledge at the time) then you should be at peace with yourself – nobody could have done more in your shoes.

Another, more positive, piece of advice is about enjoying the good moments. Even when times are relatively bleak there will undoubtedly be good moments to savour – it may be a birthday, a few hours sat together in a garden, the get together of family or friends etc. Whatever it may be in your situation I recommend you stop and consciously take the opportunity to register in your mind that this is one of those "better times". When asked, dad always used to say that he didn't have good and bad days but good days and better days! Enjoy such times to the full rather than just letting them pass you by whilst you are worrying about the next issue or thing you have to do. At the end of the day these times will form part of the more comforting memories that you take forward with you when the person is no longer here.

The aspect of communication features large in the situation of caring for someone and their deterioration and passing. It is not only the external communication with supportive parties such as doctors and nurses that is key, but also the internal communication between the family and friends closely involved in the person's care. With seeing each other virtually every day Jacqueline and I had the benefit of being able to experience the changing situations together and understood mum and dad's medical and other needs. Having the ability to discuss these matters face to face was definitely an overall benefit, but other people going through similar experiences may need to resort to different types of communication (especially if there is some physical dis-tance between them, or a multitude of family involved). Fortunately nowadays we have the benefit of technol-ogy in the form of mobile phones, texting and email etc., so close contact can be maintained even if people are physically not together. Also, email can be particu-larly useful as a medium to set out thoughts, proposals and resolve differences of opinion in a more considered, less confrontational and emotionally charged way.

On the odd occasion when Jacqueline and I had a heated argument over an issue I did decide to resort to email afterwards as I found that in the middle of such a tense and stressful time trying to talk about certain sensitive issues face to face just ended up with a major argument (not productive for anyone). In such cases, the ability to calm down and set out clearly one's thoughts, views and suggestions was far more productive. Such an approach allows both parties to fully set out how they feel (without interruption and escalation) and even if a common agreement cannot be reached at least both parties feel they have had the opportunity to fully express their views and position, which contributes to diffusing the situation. My advice is simple, albeit not always easy – whatever the situation it is essential to find a way to communicate with those involved and to always keep such communication lines open.

On a very different topic I would like to touch on the gradual realisation, through the experience of such troubled times, of the individuality of parents. It is probably something that the majority of siblings don't really consciously think about or appreciate – especially during their earlier years. What I mean by that is that as a son or daughter you tend to grow up thinking about your mother and father as two strands of the same entity – parents. Although you realise they are individuals there is a tendency to view them in relation to you i.e. as *your* parents rather than two individual human beings (not blood related), who have the same hopes, fears, needs and frailties as yourself as an individual.

When people are ill and need support it is much easier to concentrate on, and default to, the physical issues at hand and look to deal with those, often missing (or minimising) the emotional needs of the person involved as an individual. Those emotional needs can run the complete spectrum from engaging a religious leader to just spending time holding the person's hand or asking them how they feel about a current situation and what they would like to do. This area is something that needs particular cognisance when one parent passes away. Try to imagine that you are eighty eight and had been married to someone for say fifty eight years (and therefore spent most of your life together) and then you suddenly lost them – how would you feel? It is not just the initial loss and emptiness but all the myriad of day to day things that you would miss – holding their hand in bed at night (now the bed's empty), reminiscing about old mutual experiences, the physical contact of a kiss etc. Being able to support someone practically in such circumstances is one thing (e.g. ensuring they have a home, are fed and have any other basic support necessary) but the need to ameliorate the individual emotional elements is a far more difficult task. It is only when you try to put yourself in that same situation of loss that you physically start to feel inside the pain that would be there and that your mum or dad is now having to carry with them every day.

I suppose talking about pain and suffering inevitably raises the topic of religion and the existence and role of a supreme being (whatever that may mean to you). You may feel from reading this book that I am a fairly religious person, but that is not really so. Obviously, I was brought up and received all the appropriate education in the Jewish religion, being taught Hebrew and having my *"Barmitzvah"* (coming of age) at the age of thirteen as normal. I understand the tenants of the religion and the various traditions and ways but I cannot say I practice the religion day to day. The adherence to all the various requirements I have referred to in previous chapters are mainly out of respect for mum and dad and their strong religious beliefs (i.e. wanting to maximise my love and respect for them). If anything, the experiences around the last phases of their lives would bring me to question any faith I did have even further. Consideration of the lives that Ian and Fay led, their strong adherence to religious beliefs, their constant striving and innate values in terms of helping other people and being "good people" themselves only raises the question more strongly in my mind – how could a benign supreme being allow such pain and suffering to take place (particularly with dad over such a long period). It has certainly shaken what little faith I may have had to start with. The words from the song *"Tell me there's a heaven"* by the artist Chris Rea echo in my mind:

"… Tell me there's a heaven;
Tell me that it's true;
Tell me there's a reason;
Why I'm seeing what I do..".

I am sure a number of readers with strong faith would be able to "explain" why such situations arise, but for the moment the experiences of the last few years have only added to the conundrum and challenges I face in coming to terms with the nature of my parents' deaths and my own mortality going forward.

In a similar vein I sometimes question the achievements my parents experienced. When you ponder on the end phases of their lives it is understandable to question what the point of all the hard work and achievements was over so many years – look where it led to in the end. It is a natural reaction to question such things and I suppose at the end of the day it comes back to a fundamental determination to make the best of whatever time you may have, rather than dwelling on the end over which we have no control. Certainly there has been a more acute realisation of the important things in life. Seeing both mum and dad lying in bed close to their respective deaths brought home the obvious fact that at those key stages in life it does not matter what material possessions you have. A big house or flash car are of no use whatsoever when you are reduced by illness to that low level. The only real benefits at such a time are the love, support and care of family and friends – it is people and relationships that are the real wealth in a person's life. If you are fortunate to be able to enjoy material items as they come your way then all well and good, as long as the really important aspects of life are nurtured and not forgotten or sacrificed.

Another implication of the losses is that they have probably made me more acutely aware of my age and heightened the anxiety and fear in relation to medical problems. As mentioned earlier there is a natural anxiety (and fear) now in terms of when (not if) I will experience medical issues which cannot be fully cured (as in the past) and will move me into the scenario that mum and dad had to deal with in their later lives. Without sending out a view of total "doom and gloom" there is bound to be something that occurs at some stage that

RUSSELL HARRIS

proves to be fatal – that is an inevitability! I suppose in response I fall back on an extract from the poem "*Desiderata*" by Max Erhmann, which says:

"...... *Take kindly the council of the years, gracefully surrendering the things of youth. .... Nurture the strength of spirit to shield you in sudden misfortune. But do not distress yourself with imaginings. Many fears are born of fatigue and loneliness. ..... And whether or not it is clear to you, no doubt the universe is unfolding as it should. Therefore be at peace with God, whatever you conceive him to be...*".

Also a potential implication of parental (or any close) loss can be the movement towards a more negative and critical outlook on life and situations. It is probably understandable if you perceive this as a possible materialisation and outlet of the pain and anger felt as a result of the loss. It is something worth consciously looking out for and trying to address in such situations.

The memories of loved ones gone can be both painful and comforting depending on the timing involved. As mentioned before, trying to talk about the person early on in the bereavement period can be extremely upsetting and uncomfortable, whilst reminiscing (especially re the good times) after a period of time has passed can be helpful and comforting. It ensures that their lives and impact on other people are not forgotten, but live on. Trying to move your mind to remember more of the pleasant memories, rather than those around the end of their lives, is something worth pursuing.

I suppose this draws to a close everything I want to say at this stage. This book has set out the unique, individual story of the last ten years of my life; the final phases of the lives of my dear, wonderful parents Ian and Fay; their sad passing from this world and the struggle of myself (and my sister Jacqueline) in coping with the challenges and pain that has generated. Hopefully this has resonated with those of you who have experienced a similar loss and that my observations, reflections and suggestions have either proved to be helpful or will be so for those of you yet to face such trials and tribulations. I have looked to bridge the gap between one of the most individual experiences in a person's life and the generic universality of such situations. I wish you well in whatever faces you in the future and hope that this journey has been helpful in some way.

For those of you who knew Fay and Ian my hope is that this book may help to consolidate memories of those special people and for the rest of you that you now know a little about the "Harris family" of Fay, Ian, Jacqueline and Russell.

I want to conclude by wishing you the strength, support, peace of mind and serenity to deal with your individual challenges of a similar nature in the future. Have a good life and find peace, whatever that may mean to you.

- - - - - - - - -

www.ingramcontent.com/pod-product-compliance
Lightning Source LLC
La Vergne TN
LVHW091249080426
835510LV00007B/174